For Clint McCann

ut unum sint

—Bill Eerdmans

AN EERDMANS CENTURY

AN EERDMANS CENTURY

1911–2011

———

by

Larry ten Harmsel

with

Reinder Van Til

WILLIAM B. EERDMANS PUBLISHING COMPANY

GRAND RAPIDS, MICHIGAN / CAMBRIDGE, U.K.

© 2011 Wm. B. Eerdmans Publishing Co.

Published 2011 by
Wm. B. Eerdmans Publishing Co.
2140 Oak Industrial Drive N.E., Grand Rapids, Michigan 49505 /
P.O. Box 163, Cambridge CB3 9PU U.K.

Printed in the United States of America

17 16 15 14 13 12 11   7 6 5 4 3 2 1

Library of Congress Cataloging-in-Publication Data

Ten Harmsel, Larry, 1945-
An Eerdmans century: 1911-2011 / by Larry ten Harmsel with Reinder Van Til.
        p.   cm.
ISBN 978-0-8028-6658-5 (cloth: alk. paper)
1. Wm. B. Eerdmans Publishing Co. — History.
2. Christian literature — Publishing — United States — History.
3. Publishers and publishing — United States — History.
4. Book industries and trade — United States — History.
5. Booksellers and bookselling — United States — History.
I. Van Til, Reinder.   II. Title.

BV2369.5.U6T46   2011
070.5088'280409730904 — dc23
                                                    2011032721

www.eerdmans.com

Contents

Contents

Acknowledgments

———

Many people helped me search for documents relating to the early history of the Eerdmans Publishing Company, making that part of the process both pleasant and productive. I would especially like to thank Dick Harms, the Archivist at Calvin College; Geoffrey Reynolds, Archivist for the Holland Joint Historical Archives; Sharon Carlson, Archivist at Western Michigan University; Elton Bruins, of the Van Raalte Institute; and Daniel Vaca, a doctoral candidate at Columbia University. Within the Eerdmans Company, I am especially indebted to Jann Myers, Willem Mineur, and Claire VanderKam for their ability to locate old photos and musty mementos; and to Linda Bieze for her efficiency at putting together all the pieces.

LtH

Introduction

Founded in 1911, the William B. Eerdmans Publishing Company celebrates its 100th year of existence in 2011. Such longevity is unusual in the American business climate: more than two-thirds of family-owned businesses disappear before fifty years have passed, and fewer than one in twenty survive for a century. As a family business, in other words, the company has achieved something rare.

In another respect, however, what it has done is not only rare — it's unprecedented. No other corporation in America has endured (and prospered) for a century with only two leaders — the founder, William Bernard Eerdmans Sr., who ran things from 1911 until 1963, and his son, William Bernard Eerdmans Jr., who took over in 1963 and continues as president in 2011. Ralph Waldo Emerson says an institution is the lengthened shadow of one man; in many ways, Eerdmans Publishing Company is the lengthened shadow of two men.

That two Bill Eerdmanses have run the company for a century may be suitable for an entry in Ripley's *Believe It or Not* or a line in the *Guinness Book of World Records,* but in fact it means very little by itself. What it underscores, however, is the perseverance, determination, and effectiveness of a certain vision of life. Both men lived long and remained engaged with their work. Both men believed in encouraging a religious understanding of human enterprise without descending into dogmatism. Both of them saw their Christianity as a way to engage — not escape — the world and its troubles.

Over the course of a century, the issues and approaches have changed. Problems, ideas, names, and faces have changed. The determination to confront them has not. A serious publishing house is neither a purveyor nor an underminer of orthodoxy; it is a forum for ideas. Openness to ideas has been the legacy of these two Eerdmans publishers through ten decades.

From the publisher: Bill Eerdmans' initial entry on EerdWord, the corporate blog

At dinner — my first with Jimmy Dunn, ace *Neutestamentler* from the University of Durham — Jimmy (always "Jimmy") asked me if we had a mission statement. This surprised me, as it sounded a bit like the suspicions of a cagey fundamentalist, though of course I knew better. To his surprise, I said we had none but that he should be able to find one unhidden in plain view in our catalogs, "speaking volumes."

That was about thirty years ago (I could be off by a decade or two). But for retrofitting, for time and circumstance, our catalogs, brother, I said, are cut from the same cloth: one hundred years of a pledge to sow the seeds of faith and culture *sub specie aeternitatis* — under the aspect of eternity. And so it goes from book to book, each in its own way a blessing. Thanks to you, Jimmy, and to the chorus of your fellow witnesses who have given us a mission statement so exquisite it's almost too much to believe or bear.

Deo volente,
William B. Eerdmans Jr.

A Nest of Eleven

In his later life, William B. Eerdmans Sr. often talked about his birthplace and family in the Netherlands. His favorite description of where he came from, often repeated, began with the expression "a nest of eleven." At the most literal level he was talking about his family, but he may well have had other nests in mind. There were eleven provinces in the Netherlands. There were eleven cities in the province of Friesland, where he was born. His parents, Bernardus Dirk Eerdmans (1844-1901) and Dirkje Pars (1848-1929), raised eleven children in the Frisian city of Bolsward. All these nests of eleven were somewhat tangled places in which to live.

For most of the nineteenth and twentieth centuries, the Netherlands comprised eleven provinces. That was an accidental number: those governmental entities emerged haphazardly from medieval counties or duchies and joined together in a modern state only after the Napoleonic era. Before that, there had been seventeen united provinces in the Netherlands. The creation of Belgium and the religious wars of the sixteenth century altered the borders. So the number eleven took on a certain importance to Netherlanders. Like the original Thirteen Colonies in the United States, these provinces lay claim to an illustrious history. (A twelfth province, Flevoland, consisting mostly of polders reclaimed from the sea, was created in 1986, but it will need centuries to acquire the patina of historical grandeur accruing to the older eleven.)

Governments in Amsterdam and The Hague have long considered Friesland to be merely another province, one of eleven. Holland, the province in which both Amsterdam and The Hague reside, imagines itself to be the most important — the primus inter pares. After all, even the country is sometimes called Holland, the most populous province coming to symbolize the entire nation by a process of synecdoche.

Frisians, however, don't buy it. They often think of themselves as an independent nation. Never conquered by the Romans, who occupied territories just south of Friesland, they are proud of their fierce history. After Charlemagne granted the country independence in the eighth century, its laws insisted, in ringing poetry, that "all Frisians should be fully free, the born and the unborn, so long as the wind blows from the skies, so long as the child cries, so long as grass grows green and flowers bloom, so long as the sun rises and the world stands." They have a long tradition of independent — some would say fractious and wayward — behavior; a language that is distinct from Dutch; a rich literary tradition descended from, or at least related to, Nordic sagas; an immensely productive farming industry; hardy breeds of horses and cattle; and flat green fields crisscrossed by irrigation ditches and canals, swarming with sheep and other livestock.

Friesland also has a long history of international commerce. By the early fifteenth century, its capital, Leeuwarden, was a Hansa city, as were the nearby free cities of Stavoren, Dokkum, and others. In 1412, Bolsward became a member of the Hanseatic League as well. The merchants of Bolsward, in concert with other Frisian cities, hoped to circumvent the Dutch political and commercial centers of Amsterdam, Rotterdam, and The Hague to the south, and to establish their own relationships with the wider world. By 1455, Bolsward obtained a city charter, and it soon took its place as one of the eleven cities of the Dutch province of Friesland. In addition to roads, the cities have long been connected by canals and waterways.

During the harsh winters of the sixteenth and seventeenth centuries, when roads were frozen and impassable, skilled ice skaters sometimes plied between the eleven cities on the network of canals. Such hardy wayfarers were celebrated in verse and story. In the early twentieth century roads and transport had been much improved, but the Frisians, in a spirit of romantic atavism, created a new competition, the *elfstedentocht* (eleven cities race). It has become one of the most popular Dutch sporting events, partly because it caters to an archaic national mythology, and partly because it is dauntingly sporadic. The ice in the canals must be certified safe, and in the warm winters of the twentieth century conditions have seldom been right. Since 1906, the year the modern race began, it has been held only fifteen times, most recently in 1997.

By the time William Bernard Eerdmans, the seventh of eleven children, was born in Bolsward in 1882, his family had achieved a rather prominent position in the city. His great-grandfather, Dirk Hendriks Eerdmans, had been mayor of the city in 1787, in what local historians call the "Patriotic Times." Mayor Eerdmans, along with other leading citizens of Bolsward, had mounted an uprising against the dominance of the House of Orange, which later became the Dutch royal family. He and his compatriots were able to wring trading concessions from The Hague, allowing Bolsward to continue its tradition of international commerce. The patriotism for which they are celebrated was, of course, loyalty to Friesland, not to the Netherlands.

Growing up, Willy (as his family called him) heard many stories about his illustrious clan. Family lore often provides more anecdotal drama than historical accuracy, and yet no family can understand itself without it. Even when they're not completely verifiable, these old stories weave a fabric that the family comes to accept as its own. The history becomes emotionally true even if some of the details may be fanciful. The Eerdmans family in Bolsward believed itself to have come from France, where in the seventeenth century the Edict of Nantes gave a wide range of civil rights to French Protestants, followers of John Calvin.

When Louis XIV revoked the Edict in 1685, the family fled France, along with an estimated 400,000 other Protestants. They were afraid that in the renewed spirit of intolerance there would be another series of ruinous religious wars in France, and they were determined to hold on to their religion, even if it meant the loss of their homeland. Many of these diaspora Calvinists were skilled craftsmen with a tradition of intellectual independence. They possessed the talents and economic means to pursue life in new surroundings. First, it seems, the Eerdmans family went into Germany, where they picked up a Germanic name. Then they traveled farther and farther north, finally settling in Dutch (rather than German) Friesland, whose culture had acquired a strong Calvinist cast. Early members of the family had been silversmiths, farmers, butchers, and traders, and they maintained some international contacts with fellow Huguenots and with coreligionists they had come to know and trust during their long flight from France.

Willy's father, Bernardus, owned a textile factory that had originally tanned hides from the area's slaughterhouses and processed wool from the extensive sheep farms. Both leather and wool had been important export products since at least the time of the medieval Hansa traders, who had taken them from the western end of Europe and exchanged them for timber and other goods more common in the east. The Eerdmans *textielfabriek* employed about fifty workers during Willy's childhood, selling its products throughout Europe, and acquiring an increasing amount of its raw materials from sources beyond the provincial borders.

By the time Willy was in his teens, several of his older siblings had decamped from Bolsward to the United States. His oldest brother, Dirk (1878-1946), moved to Paterson, New Jersey, in 1896 at the age of eighteen. There he established an import business that sold items such as Droste chocolates, Verkade biscuits, Haarlemmer oil, and other products from the Netherlands to the extensive community of Dutch immigrants in the area.

Some time later, Willy's sister Trijn came to New Jersey to visit, and she met Dirk's sometime business partner, Herman Hamstra, a Frisian immigrant living in Clifton, near Paterson. Before long she married Hamstra, and the couple remained in the United States,

The women of WBE's family: *seated,* **Dirkje Pars Eerdmans (mother), Catherine Eerdmans Vander Laan (sister);** *standing,* **Trijn Eerdmans (sister), Bertha Eerdmans Schaafsma (sister), ca. 1927**

where her husband sold a line of imported products to immigrants and others in the greater New York City area.

In the very late 1890s, Dirk Eerdmans moved to Grand Rapids, Michigan, to continue his business within the large Dutch colony there. As part of his trade, he collaborated with his brother-in-law Hobbe Vander Laan, who was married to the family's oldest daughter, Catherine. The Vander Laans continued to live in Paterson; but as a partner of his east coast brother-in-law, Dirk sold Bibles and religious books in western Michigan, books that had been sent to Vander Laan by a publisher in Franeker, Friesland. For the commu-

5

nity of committed Dutch Calvinists in America, religious books in their ancestral tongue held a strong appeal: they preserved a whiff of the homeland in the maelstrom of the New World.

Dirk Eerdmans wasn't the only bookseller in Grand Rapids at the turn of the century. As early as 1909, Louis Kregel had opened a store that sold religious books; and Brant Sevensma billed himself as a *boekhandelaar en uitgever* (bookseller and publisher) from his shop on East (later Eastern) Avenue. Indeed, there were dozens of ministers, students, and recent immigrants who found ways to sell new and used books to the intensely religious community in West Michigan.

By 1914, as it happened, Hobbe Vander Laan had saved enough money to retire. He later told a nephew that he'd amassed about 120,000 guilders in just under twenty years of bookselling. He returned to the Netherlands with his wife, Willy's sister Catherine, bought a patrician home in Driebergen, near Utrecht, and continued raising his eight children in the land of his birth. The prosperity he was able to generate in the book trade must have been of considerable interest to the youthful brother-in-law who would later become not only a bookseller but a publisher.

Another one of Willy's sisters, Petronella, lived in South Dakota with her husband, a man named Korperhoek. She would later divorce him, marry Louis Zondervan, and take up residence in the Grand Rapids area. Two of the Korperhoek sons, who took the surname Zondervan when they were adopted by their stepfather, were to play a significant role in their Uncle Willy's later life. Another sister, Froukje, married Jan Anema some years later, and moved to western Canada, where the couple lived in the small community of Neerlandia, Alberta.

With several of their siblings already in North America, apparently finding ways to thrive in their new surroundings, Willy and his slightly older brother, Johannes (called Jo), also nursed thoughts about emigration. Jo dropped out of school at the age of sixteen and petitioned his father for permission to join his older brother and sisters in the New World.

Bernardus would not hear of it. It may have seemed to him that his large family was orbiting too far from its Frisian roots, that his own failing health required more sons to work in the business; or he may simply have concluded that Johannes was not mature enough to embark on such a journey. In any case, he was vociferous in his opposition. Either Jo should go to school or he should continue working for his father to gain some maturity and experience. Then maybe they could talk about it again after a couple of years had passed. So Jo went to work alongside Willy, who was both a dutiful student and an employee of his father's firm.

And then came a family trauma — another departure, of a dramatically different kind. Every Thursday, Willy and Jo took the train to Rotterdam, where they would purchase a week's supply of skins for the family's tannery. For some reason, Willy, the younger son, routinely carried the cash needed for the purchase, some 300 guilders. His father had apparently placed a measure of trust in him despite his relative youth. In any event, on one of these trips to Rotterdam in 1898, Willy asked his brother Jo to take the list of needed inventory along with the money to purchase it.

Willy had met a girl on one of his previous trips to Rotterdam, and he wanted to see her again. It was to be something of a lark for him, a day of playing corporate hooky. He was sure his older brother could handle the purchases, which were to be a routine replacement for the leather they had processed and sold in the previous week. The brothers agreed to meet late in the afternoon at Central Station on the bank of the Delft River, under the big clock, to catch the train home. The skins would be shipped separately by the company's agent in Rotterdam.

Willy gave the cash to Jo and headed off to find his girlfriend. At the end of the afternoon he went to the station to wait for his brother. But Jo did not show up. The late afternoon faded into evening, and Willy became increasingly distraught. He ran to the shipping agent and found that no skins had been purchased. When he returned to the station there was still no sign of Jo. Willy finally caught a late train for what must have been a terrible ride home. He had neglected his duties, had split up with his brother, had spent the day with a girl, and now he was returning without his brother or the skins or the money — and with no idea of what had happened.

The police in Rotterdam got involved in the mystery, but their search turned up nothing. The family placed advertisements in newspapers, looked wherever they could imagine there might be a sign of Jo, and found nothing. It was a frantic, harrowing time for all of them, with emotions riding high and sinking low. And Willy, who had neglected to perform his duties in Rotterdam, must have felt a special burden of responsibility for this tragedy.

After a month or so the police and the family concluded that Johannes had likely been the victim of an accident — or of some kind of violence. He'd been carrying 300 guilders, a sizable amount of money. Rotterdam was a huge seaport, with ships and crews from all over the world crowding its docks. The port, like many others, sported a reputation for roughness, hard living, and occasional brawls. Jo, they imagined, might have been beaten by assailants, he might have been tossed into the harbor — almost anything might have happened to him. But since they could find no trace of him, it seemed clear that he had died.

The Eerdmans family went into mourning. Willy's mother and sisters wore black; the church held a funeral service; the community mourned the passing of one of its own. Willy's father struggled to contain his anger with the guilt-ridden son who had returned alive; at the same time he nursed his sadness for the son who was departed. Bernardus and his son Jo had not seen eye to eye. But their old arguments must have seemed petty in retrospect, now that he was gone. Willy, as a good Calvinist, carefully attuned to the theology of guilt, felt his father's anguish very deeply. He was in disgrace. And of course he, too, was in mourning.

Not so with Jo. He had taken the 300 guilders from Willy on a Thursday morning, and by noon he'd gone to the offices of the Holland-America Line, on an island in the middle of the lazily flowing Rhine River, where he booked a ticket to New York. That would have cost him about 50 guilders, though there is no way to be certain what he paid. The boat sailed on Friday morning. About two weeks later Jo was in New York City, nearly penniless, according to what he later told the family. He did not remember the address of his sister, who lived in nearby Paterson, New Jersey. Nor did he think to go to the thriving Dutch community just across the river and simply ask around, which might well have brought him to her house. On the other hand, it is quite possible that he had plenty of money left and wanted to lie low for a while, knowing what kind of trouble he was in.

Fortunately, he remembered the address in Michigan of his older brother Dirk. Jo later told the family that he spent the next two months selling newspapers and doing other odd jobs in New York to amass enough money for a train ticket to Grand Rapids. He finally went there, found his brother's house, sat on the front stoop, and waited for Dirk to come home from work. Initially pleased and surprised to see his little brother, Dirk exploded when he found out what had happened. Three months had gone by, and Jo had somehow not managed to send a note to his family explaining what he had done. They sent off a cable immediately, informing the family of Jo's whereabouts.

Afraid of the consequences should he return home, Jo remained in Grand Rapids, where he started a dairy business. He didn't go back to Bolsward for a visit with his family until 1910, by which time he had married and moved to Pease, Minnesota. He never saw his father again; by 1910 Bernardus had been gone for almost a decade.

Willy, meanwhile, had to go back to work in the family business. The atmosphere in the office must have been thick with recriminations, but he soldiered on. He thought himself an important part of the enterprise: a diligent, conscientious junior executive despite his youth. However, in 1900 his brother Dirk returned from America. Bernardus, in failing health, had asked the eldest son to come back home and take over the management of the family enterprises, both the textile division and the tannery.

In later life, Willy tried not to resent this thickening of the familial atmosphere, but with his brother's return, he apparently decided that it was time for him to decamp to America. His father died in

1901. Shortly thereafter, Willy asked for his mother's permission to leave. He and his mother were emotionally close, and at first she did not want to let him go. Then she said it would be all right if he went, but only for a visit — to see his family. And that was how they left it for a while. In 1901, he made the first of what would become many Atlantic crossings and, despite what his mother hoped or believed, he was determined to stay — to find or make his way in America.

Coming to America

I n 1901, soon after the death of his father, Willy left Bolsward for good. He told his mother that he wanted to visit his sisters and brother in America, but his intention was always to stay there once he got there. At nineteen years of age he was fluent in German, English, Dutch, and Frisian, with more than a smattering of French as well. He was filled with energy and ideas. He had no doubt that he would be able to make his way in the world. The family business, under the guidance of his eldest brother, Dirk, must have provided some of the money that allowed him to cross the Atlantic, but he seldom went anywhere empty-handed. He was already something of an independent entrepreneur, always buying and selling one or another product, and very likely he had money of his own as well as the family contribution to his welfare. Although documentary records about these years are scarce, his ability to return from the United States to Europe regularly suggests that, at the very least, he was not impecunious.

One of his sisters was married to a bookseller in Michigan, another to an importer of Dutch foodstuffs in New Jersey, and Willy had learned a great deal about commerce in the company of his father. Even though their time together had not been long in years, he was a quick study, and he had picked up a great deal.

Arriving at the Hoboken docks in 1901, he was met by his sister Catherine, Mrs. Hobbe Vander Laan, and he stayed with her family in nearby Paterson. Soon, in letters that he sent home, he convinced his mother that he should be allowed to stay in the United States. While in New Jersey, and later in Grand Rapids, Willy joined the Christian Reformed Church, a Calvinist denomination that was at that time composed almost entirely of Dutch immigrants and their offspring. Willy was a strongly committed Calvinist, so his affiliation with this group is not surprising, except for one thing: his father had strongly opposed this splinter group in the Netherlands. The Christian Reformed Church was part of a movement, the Gereformeerde Kerk, that, in two nineteenth-century secessions, had broken away from the state church of the Netherlands, the Reformed (Hervormde) Church.

Bernardus Eerdmans had often told his children that he had used his influence to save more than eighty churches in Friesland from splitting with the mother church. In the mid-1880s a group of conservative Dutch Calvinists began agitating for separation from the state church, which they said had fallen prey to Enlightenment liberalism. Hundreds of churches throughout the country joined the schismatic group, the *Doleantie*. Willy's father was proud that he had diminished that number whenever he could. He wanted to see a unified Christian church, not a series of increasingly hostile splinter groups. But the new church, whose members called themselves the *dolerende* (Latin for "sorrowing"), did indeed break away. By 1892 the dissenters had joined with the Christian Reformed Church to form the Reformed Churches in the Netherlands.

The new church was led by the charismatic polymath Abraham Kuyper, who had founded the Free University of Amsterdam in 1880, where he became a distinguished professor of theology. In 1898, Kuyper delivered the Stone Lectures at Princeton University, bringing his ideas about Calvinist Christianity to a wide American audience. By 1901 he had been chosen prime minister of the Netherlands, a position he held until 1906. Kuyper, whom Willy's father saw as something of a nemesis, was clearly a hero to Bernardus's son. It was the Kuyperian church that he joined in America, and within a few years he would be attending a Kuyperian college in Grand Rapids.

For his first few months in America, Willy taught in a Christian Reformed day school. His fluency in both Dutch and English, the result of superb educational institutions in Bolsward, made him a good choice for this community. Immigrant Hollanders had managed to hold on to many aspects of their Dutch culture, but they were always clear about one thing: their children must learn English, the language of their new home. The schools in these immigrant enclaves sometimes hired teachers who spoke only English; but someone like Willy, fluent in both tongues, would have been to their liking.

After a summer of teaching, though, he decided that it was time to move on. He transplanted himself to Grand Rapids, which had become the hub of a sizable Dutch *kolonie*. Albertus Van Raalte (1811-1876), a dissenting pastor from an earlier Dutch schism (an irreverent but often accurate slogan: "two Dutchmen, a church; three Dutchmen, a heresy"), had founded the city of Holland, Michigan, in 1847. Other Dutch immigrant communities — Zeeland, Overisel, Vriesland, Harlem, Drenthe, Borculo — had followed in short order. Over the ensuing half century many of these people and their offspring had settled in Grand Rapids, which despite its ethnic diversity eventually became the anchor of the large West Michigan *kolonie,* nearly a third of its population arising from Netherlandic roots.

In Grand Rapids, Willy established a small import company with Herman Hamstra (who would later move to Clifton, New Jersey, and marry Willy's sister Trijn). His brother Dirk had lived in Grand Rapids for several years before returning to Bolsward; his disgraced brother, Jo, had owned a dairy in Grand Rapids before moving to Minnesota. Thus the community must have seemed in many ways like an extension of home. There were entire neighborhoods in Grand Rapids that thought of themselves as reconstituted provinces of the "old country," and, judging from their surnames, at least two of Willy's business partners in his early years — Hamstra and Sevensma — were Frisian.

Although records of this period of his life are scarce, Willy seems to have enrolled in 1904 in the institution that would become Calvin

College and Seminary. In that era Calvin taught classes in both Dutch and English, depending on the professor and the subject. Willy retained many pleasant memories of his studies. Over the remainder of his life he contributed a great deal to the college, both financially and in personal involvement on many of the college's boards and committees. He donated the German pipe organ, at a cost of $30,000, that provided music for Calvin's chapel services from 1929 to the mid-1960s, when the college relocated to the Knollcrest campus on the outskirts of Grand Rapids. He donated the funds that created the Calvin Foundation. He enriched the archives with an extensive collection of Albertus Van Raalte documents. He even cowrote an official Calvin College song.

In the early years of the twentieth century, Calvin was a small school: eight men and one woman were in Willy's graduating class in 1908. Years later, reminiscing about his student years, he said that a bus ride would cost him a nickel, the price of a good cigar. Willy loved a good cigar, so he avoided the bus as much as possible. He often rode a bicycle around town, and from twin baskets on the back he peddled books to his fellow students, as well as to pastors and families that showed an interest in theological or devotional literature. Most of those books were in Dutch, probably overstocked items from his brother-in-law Hobbe Vander Laan, or items he had acquired himself on overseas buying trips. In a 1965 interview with the historian Herbert Brinks, he talks about returning to the Netherlands four or five times during those early years. He would visit his widowed mother and his remaining siblings in Bolsward. He imported blankets and items of clothing from the family's textile factory, and he also made forays into cities, where he would buy books, chocolates, and other products he and his partner Herman Hamstra could sell in the immigrant enclaves of West Michigan.

With all these peripatetic activities, Willy was never a typical student, nor, by his own admission, a particularly intellectual one. But he worked hard and kept busy. When he graduated from the college in 1908, he had every intention of going on to become a pastor in the Christian Reformed Church, which would have required another

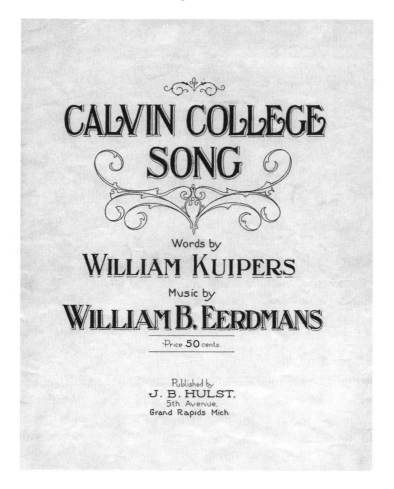

**Sheet music for the Calvin College Song,
music composed by WBE**

two or three years of study. The great majority of Dutch immigrants
who came to West Michigan were impoverished peasants and farmers from the agricultural provinces of the Netherlands. In marked
contrast, Willy's cosmopolitan sensibilities, his wide experience in
travel and trade, his sophisticated educational background, and the
prosperous situation of his family in Bolsward must have made him
an exceptional figure in the community.

**The John Calvin Junior College graduating class of 1908
(WBE is in the front row, far right)**

Before embarking on his seminary education, he decided to take a trip to Europe and solemnly informed the *Grand Rapids Press* of his intentions. The following appeared in the society column of Tuesday, June 16, 1908 (p. 6):

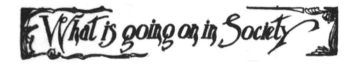

W. Eerdmans of the fourth literary class at the John Calvin Junior college left yesterday for Holland where he will make an extended visit with relatives and friends. Mr. Eerdmans will also make a tour of Europe before returning, visiting Switzerland, France, and Germany.

When he returned to Friesland to visit his family in 1908, he would have found many changes in the family and the community. His oldest brother, Dirk, had taken over management of the textile factory and the tannery. His brother Matthijs had purchased a tobacco store in the city and was developing a significant business for himself not simply selling cigars, cigarettes, and related products, but also importing tobacco from foreign markets. By the beginning of World War I, Thijs would virtually corner the market for cigars in Europe and would become an extremely wealthy man.

In 1908 the city of Bolsward was still a seaport, as it had been for centuries, but that privileged situation was not to last for long. The Dutch government in Amsterdam was planning to build an immense dike, cutting off the Zuider Zee (now renamed the Ijsselmeer, or Ijssel Lake) from the North Sea. The shallow offshore waters near Bolsward were to be drained and turned into farmland. Before long the city would retain only a small shipping channel that would connect it not to the oceans of the world but only to a big Dutch lake.

Willy was once again confirmed in the notion that he (and several of his siblings) had made the right decision when they moved to America. He exuded a strong and meticulous sense of who he was and of where he wanted his life to be directed. His religious convictions impelled him to serve God, while his business background and connections seemed to push in a more secular direction. He was not satisfied with the import business that he and Hamstra were pursuing; besides, Hamstra wanted to move to the east coast, where there was a far larger population base. So the partnership broke up.

Willy decided he would serve God in the most forthright and direct way possible: as a minister of the gospel. In the fall of 1908 he went back into school and pursued a seminarian's course of study. His son, Bill Jr., remembers hearing about those days from his father when he was younger:

My father worked his way through college and seminary by importing goods such as vases and blankets from the Netherlands and Germany and selling them to fellow immigrants in western Michigan. Because of his interest in theology and things spiritual, he added books to the goods he was importing, both books in the Dutch language and books in English.

Dutch Calvinists, no matter what their occupation, were known to read theology and biblical studies as though they were part of their daily bread. But my father also sold them books in English (somehow or another he was importing those books from England at the time), because those immigrants were also serious about learning the language of their new home and becoming Americanized.

In later life the elder Mr. Eerdmans told several stories about how and why he left the seminary after just one year. The stories have different emphases, but they all point to a growing recognition that his life would be best spent doing something other than preaching and ministering to a congregation. Several of his stories had to do with the experience of preaching.

Seminarians were expected to learn by doing, and his first preaching assignment took place in a farming community in the northern part of Michigan. He traveled there on Saturday and was put up by a farm family. On Sunday morning he preached a sermon in English; the midday sermon he preached in Dutch — for people who were more comfortable in that language; and the evening sermon was once again in English. He had worked long and hard preparing those three presentations, and he remembers being quite nervous beforehand. But by the end of a long Sunday he thought things had gone pretty well. As he walked back to the farm in the company of his host, the farmer said to him, "I'll bet that's the easiest five dollars you ever earned, isn't it?" The clear implication that people who didn't sweat or develop calluses weren't really working bothered Willy immensely. He never thought about the amount of pay, he insisted, but he knew he had worked extremely hard that day. If his seed was going to fall on such fallow soil — a parishioner who esteemed it so little — he'd have to think again about entering that profession.

Years later, he also remembered feeling uncomfortable with the attitudes he encountered in some of these churches. "While I loved to preach," he said, "I found a parochial mentality in our church, which was very critical of other denominations, insisting on a certain narrowness of thought. It became clear to me that the Lord had not laid me in the cradle to become a minister of the Christian Reformed Church."

There were more obstacles. His professors didn't exactly imagine his future the same way he did when he entered the seminary. His son recalls:

> While my father was pursuing his theological studies, and seeking to balance them with his importing entrepreneurship, which was paying his bills, it apparently became clear where his true talents lay. In later years he told us, with some amusement, that one of his seminary professors approached him in the wake of a seminary class he had not particularly excelled in, and said to him something like: "For a preacher, you'd make a real good salesman." This professor clearly respected my father's ability to get those Dutch and English volumes of theology into the hands of other students whose gifts lay in a more academic direction. This gentle nudge apparently helped convince him that he should drop out of seminary, and since he already had been developing a flourishing import business all along, he pursued that in earnest as a means of making a living.

In 1909, after one additional year of study, during which he toyed with the idea of pursuing a career in medicine or law, William B. Eerdmans left his seminary studies and took another trip to the Netherlands. He remembered doing a lot of thinking and praying about his future. He paid a visit to the prominent Princeton theologian Benjamin Warfield (1851-1921), an American friend and supporter of Abraham Kuyper. As WBE recalled it years later, Warfield told him that he was "taking this thing altogether too seriously." There were many things he could do that would serve the Lord — preaching wasn't the only possibility.

From Princeton, WBE sailed to the Netherlands, where he arranged a meeting with another of his heroes of the faith, Dr. Herman Bavinck (1854-1921). In 1902, Bavinck had succeeded the Dutch prime minister Abraham Kuyper as professor of theology at the Free University of Amsterdam. As WBE recalled it, Bavinck gave him very specific advice:

> "Honestly, you know what they really need in Grand Rapids and in America? So many Dutch people have emigrated and settled there; they need a publisher. They need a man to publish good books, like Kok does here in the city of Kampen. We don't all have to be ministers and evangelists. So think that over, young man." And I did think that over. That idea never left me. He reminded me that a real mission is carried on by the written word as well as the spoken word. And so, starting the very next summer, in June of 1910, I began my bookselling and publishing career.

He didn't quit his import business, but he began focusing increasingly on the importation of theological books from Holland and England, and by late summer of 1911 he decided to take the next step in his career.

Becoming a Publisher

William B. Eerdmans (WBE) had supported himself by selling religious books from the back of his bicycle during his years as a student at the John Calvin Junior College (which was to become Calvin College and Seminary). When he decided he was not cut out to be a minister, it made perfect sense for him to continue selling books. One of his brothers-in-law was in the process of making a small fortune as a bookseller in northern New Jersey. Besides, getting religious books into the hands of voracious Christian readers coincided with his love for God and for the community. Most Dutch immigrants in Grand Rapids still conducted a portion of their lives in the Dutch language; many of the churches held one or two services a week in the language of the old country; and many of the local businesses advertised in Dutch-language newspapers as well as English-language publications.

Although the first Dutch immigrants in West Michigan had arrived in 1847, and had largely passed away by the beginning of the twentieth century, there had been several smaller waves of immigration in the intervening years, which kept the language alive and solidified many cultural connections with the Netherlands, especially in matters of worship and theology.

Brant (Berendt) Sevensma was an established bookseller and publisher during the early years of the twentieth century in Grand Rapids. As far as can be determined, he sold and published books solely in the Dutch language, though their subjects were sometimes American. For example, one of his books (a recent acquisition of the Eerdmans corporate archives) was a slim paperback published in 1910. It describes the Christian Reformed Church's mission to the Zuni Indians in the American Southwest. Illustrated with many photographs, it details the challenges faced by missionaries in a field (infelicitously called "Heathen Missions") that had only recently been opened by the immigrant church.

Sevensma was older than WBE, but aside from that fact, knowledge of him is limited to a few memories among aging members of Eastern Avenue Christian Reformed Church, whose parents had spoken of him. In 1910 his business address was 347 South East Street. In August 1911, in a document filed with the state of Michigan, a business partnership between William B. Eerdmans and Brant Sevensma was declared, with initial capital of $20,000, approximately one-half provided by each of the partners. Depending on how relative values are calculated, $20,000 in 1911 was worth between $500,000 and two million dollars. In other words, WBE's share was a huge investment, an astonishing amount of wealth in the hands of a twenty-nine-year-old immigrant entrepreneur.

Brant Sevensma's shop eventually became the first location of the Eerdmans-Sevensma Bookstore and Publishing Company, in a low-slung building on East (now Eastern) Avenue, a short distance south of Wealthy Street. After Sevensma and WBE formed the partnership, the address was listed as 327 (rather than 347) South East Street, which remained the corporate address for about a year. In 1912 it was designated as 513-515 Eastern Avenue. The new firm had not moved; instead, Grand Rapids had changed the name of the street and its system for numbering buildings. The new street name and the new numbering system most likely denote the same structure the partners had occupied for the previous year, on Eastern Avenue near Logan, in the block across the street from Eastern Avenue Christian Reformed Church.

WBE was never content just running a bookstore, so he would take a horse and buggy and ride out to outlying areas, such as what is now the Grand Rapids suburb of Ada, which was farmland at that time, and he would sell books to the farmers — Bibles and devotional materials in both Dutch and English. As for the publishing part of the partnership, his son, Bill Jr., remembers it this way:

> The first book they actually published was by B. K. Kuiper [a professor of dogmatic theology at Calvin Seminary]: it was a semipopular biography of Martin Luther. With that, they realized that they were now in the book-publishing business.

Another early book by B. K. Kuiper was the Dutch-language *Ons Opmaken en Bouwen* ("Our Foundation and Growth"; the publisher identification was printed as Eerdmans-Sevensma Co., Uitgevers), which had been first serialized in the Christian Reformed Church's publication *The Banner* from 1911 to 1914. Another early B. K. Kuiper title, *The Church in History,* remains in print a hundred years later. The new Eerdmans-Sevensma firm also published a book entitled *Neo-Calvinism* in 1911, which made the case that Abraham Kuyper was a true neo-Calvinist.

However, a good many of the earliest Eerdmans-Sevensma publications were reprints of classic theological works by European scholars, works that were in the public domain and could thus be published without obtaining copyright permissions or paying royalties. And though many of these books had been written in Dutch and were now published untranslated by the new American publisher, their contents continued to be in great demand among the immigrants of western Michigan. Indeed, most of the early Eerdmans-Sevensma publications were books and pamphlets that they *distributed* rather than published. Those materials were specifically intended for Christian Reformed or Reformed Church groups and members in western Michigan and elsewhere throughout the United States and Canada: Sunday school lessons, patterns for sermons, commentaries on the Gospels and the Prophets, devotional pamphlets for homes and families, and so forth. There were also inspirational novels for adults and young readers. The new firm also

ARTICLES OF ASSOCIATION

OF

Erdmans - Sevensma Company

We, the undersigned, desiring to become incorporated under the provisions of Act No. 232, of the Public Acts of 1903, entitled "An act to revise and consolidate the laws providing for the incorporation of manufacturing and mercantile companies or any union of the two, and for the incorporation of companies for carrying on any other lawful business, except such as are precluded from organization under this act by its express provisions, and to prescribe the powers and fix the duties and liabilities of such corporations," and the acts amendatory thereof and supplementary thereto, do hereby make, execute and adopt the following articles of association, to-wit:

ARTICLE I.

The name assumed by this association, and by which it shall be known in law, is

Erdmans - Sevensma Company

ARTICLE II.

The purpose or purposes of this corporation are as follows:

To buy and sell, at wholesale and at retail, domestic and imported books, pamphlets, charts, pictures and all kinds of printed and illustrated matter, stationary and library supplies and the acquirement of manuscripts for publication and sale.

ARTICLE III.

The principal place at which operations are to be conducted is at *City of Grand Rapids,* in the county of *Kent,* State of *Michigan.*

ARTICLE IV.

The capital stock of the corporation hereby organized is the sum of *Twenty Thousand* (*$20,000.00*) dollars.

ARTICLE V.

The number of shares into which the capital stock is divided is *two thousand shares* of the par value of *Ten* dollars each.

ARTICLE VI.

The amount of capital stock subscribed is the sum of *Nineteen Thousand seven hundred* dollars.

ARTICLE VII.

The amount of said stock actually paid in at the date hereof is the sum of *Nineteen thousand seven hundred* dollars, of which amount ~~dollars has been paid in cash, and~~ *Nineteen thousand seven hundred* dollars has been paid in ~~other~~ property, an itemized description of which, with the valuation at which each item is taken, is as follows, viz:

The entire stock of German, English & Holland books and pamphlets owned by W. B. Erdmans, located at No. 936 Fifth avenue, Grand Rapids, Michigan, and all the furniture and fixtures used in connection therewith of the value of $7,700.00 and the entire stock of Holland and English books, wall mottoes, fountain pens, stationary and pictures owned by Brant S. Sevensma, at No. 345 S. East Street, Grand Rapids, Michigan, and the furniture and fixtures used in connection therewith of the value of $12,000.00

Incorporation papers, recto

ARTICLE VIII.

The office in the State of Michigan for the transaction of business shall be kept at

City of Grand Rapids, Michigan.

ARTICLE IX.

The term of existence of this corporation is fixed at *Thirty* years from the date hereof.

ARTICLE X.

The names of the stockholders, their respective residences and the number of shares of stock subscribed for by each are as follows:

NAMES.	RESIDENCE.	NO. OF SHARES.
Brant S. Sevensma	Grand Rapids, Mich.	1190
William B. Eerdmans	Grand Rapids, Mich.	770
Emma Sevensma	Grand Rapids, Mich.	10

Incorporation papers, verso

IN WITNESS WHEREOF, We, the parties hereby associating, for the purpose of giving legal effect to these articles, hereunto sign our names, this — 11ᵗʰ — day of _August_ A. D. 19 11.

NAMES.   NAMES.

Brant S. Sevensma
William B. Eerdmans.
Emma Sevensma

Corporate registration, recto

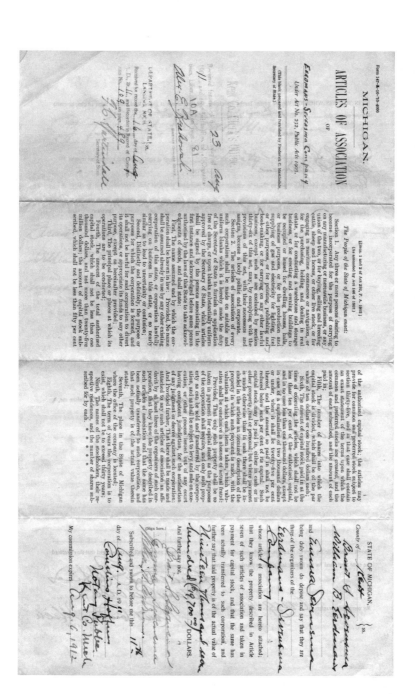

Corporate registration, verso

purchased books in Europe that were specifically intended for seminary professors and students, who would, in turn, be enlisted to disseminate these books among parish ministers throughout the denomination. WBE energetically explored every imaginable form of direct or indirect marketing within the immigrant community — and eventually well beyond it.

Early in his publishing career, WBE expressed a desire to publish a definitive edition of the works of John Calvin, the *Institutes of the Christian Religion* foremost among them. Such an undertaking would require far more capital than he could amass in those early years, but he kept his focus on the careful expression of Christian theology, especially as expressed by Abraham Kuyper and adherents of Kuyperianism; on collections of sermons and guides for the preparation of sermons; on methods of spreading the gospel; and on devotional materials for a community of people who were gradually making a cultural transition from the Dutch language to English.

WBE also kept a close eye on the secular possibilities of the Dutch-speaking marketplace in America. On April 15, 1912, the grand ship of the White Star Line, the *Titanic,* sank into the depths of the Atlantic Ocean on its maiden voyage. The loss of life aboard the great ship was instantly mourned around the world. In the space of one month, by May of 1912, WBE had himself written a 94-page book entitled *De Ramp van de Titanic (The Disaster of the Titanic),* which the new firm, less than a year old, published. Intended, as the author's preface explains, "for the circle of our Dutch people in America," it included dozens of photographs, transcripts from the initial investigations, and Dutch translations of some of the speeches given in memory of the victims and in praise of the heroes who had lost their lives while helping others. It was an amazingly quick response to what was then a very limited market: American readers of the Dutch language who wanted to know about the greatest story in the Western world that season.

The sinking of the *Titanic* (which had been called unsinkable by one of its owners) was widely viewed in religious circles as God's judgment on overweening human pride. However, WBE avoids any such explicit moralizing as he tells the story. His theological tradition and his personal sense of faith could not imagine reading God's mind, when so many innocent people had been sent to a watery grave. Instead, he talks about a lack of preparedness in the outfitting of the ship. He mentions the self-sacrificing attitude of Benjamin Guggenheim (1865-1912), the younger brother of Solomon R. and the father of Peggy (who later became an important collector of modern art). Guggenheim left a message with a survivor about his unwillingness to board a lifeboat. "No woman shall be left aboard this ship because Ben Guggenheim is a coward," he said.

Eerdmans concludes his story about this complex tragedy on a specifically religious note. He recalls the story of Jesus calming the winds on the Sea of Galilee.

> God is the only Sovereign of the sea, the only master of nature. This terrible maritime disaster shows us better than anything that the spirit of pride, the mania for speed, and the constant push for riches and renown are the curse of the world and the besetting sin of this generation. The heroic deeds and the human faithfulness of many of the men and women on board are silver linings in the dark clouds of this horrible evil [author's translation].

WBE was particularly concerned about the safety of the passenger ships that traversed the Atlantic in the early decades of the twentieth century. He made that voyage dozens of times himself, to buy books and to carry on his burgeoning import business in other products. Always the entrepreneur, he traveled back and forth regularly between America and Europe, buying blankets, vases, and books in Europe and selling them to his fellow immigrants here in the New World. In fact, at one point he took over the entire production of a small blanket factory in the Netherlands. Bill Jr. remembers:

> Some years later, when I was a fairly small boy, [my father] and I were walking around the Loop in Chicago one Sunday

afternoon when we passed Marshall Field's department store. He directed my eye into one of those famous Field's display windows and said, "There, see those — those are my blankets." I looked and, sure enough, they were the same blankets that we had at home. He had made a good sale to the Marshall Field's people.

On one of those ship passages back to the United States from one of his buying trips to Holland and Germany, my father met the young woman who was to become my mother. Paula Install was eighteen years old and en route from Germany to upstate New York to be an *au pair* for a family for a year. And even though she did not know any Dutch or Frisian or English, and had been raised a Lutheran — plus, there was an eight- or nine-year difference in their ages — the sparks from that ship meeting must have ignited a romantic flame. My father got along well enough in German to carry on conversations with her. After Paula spent a year with the family in New York, she returned home to Germany.

But WBE, on his many subsequent buying trips to Europe, would show up in Paula's hometown of Bunde, in the German province of Ostfriesland, close to the Dutch border, to visit her. He had a round, red Dutch face, and when her sisters would see him coming up the path to the Install home, they would teasingly call out, "Paula, hier kommt der Edamer Käse" ("here comes the Edam cheese").

They were married in 1917, while the Great War was still being waged, and they remained in the Netherlands for more than a year. Their first child, Ilse, was born there in 1919, shortly after the end of World War I, in Utrecht, where the small family had holed up for about a year while WBE was maintaining relationships and reconnecting with family in Europe. His brother-in-law, the retired bookseller Hobbe Vander Laan, had moved from New Jersey back to Utrecht, and the two families probably spent many fruitful hours comparing notes. WBE, Paula, and their young daughter returned to the United States in 1920, and a second daughter, Eleanor, was born in early 1921. The family made yet another trip to Europe when Eleanor was just four months old. A few entries in the diary of the eminent Dutch historian Jacob van Hinte, who was on his way to America on the Holland-America ship *Rotterdam,* capture their likeness. His entry for July 14, 1921, reads:

> Played dominoes again with the likeable Mrs. and Mr. Eerdmans in the evening. She is German, and has a pale, delicate face, beautiful blue eyes, sometimes a little sad. She speaks little, but that does not matter. On the contrary, it exudes tranquility. He: a Frisian, more noticeable by his psyche than his physique. He too projects calmness, but at the same time also great warmth, which inspires confidence. And both these quiet people live for their dear young children, and for each other, but at the same time are interested in everything outside their family circle.

On Friday, July 22, after staying for a few days in the Dutch immigrant neighborhoods of Paterson, New Jersey, van Hinte reencountered the Eerdmans family in his hotel. "Conversed until one o'clock at night with Mr. Eerdmans," he observes, "a man who is becoming increasingly attractive the longer one gets to know him."

Back in Grand Rapids, WBE continued his tremendously busy life. He and Sevensma continued to publish new titles even while distributing and selling new books published in Europe as well as reissuing older ones. He translated several books from the Dutch, and seems to have ghostwritten a couple of them, too. And he continued importing products from Europe for an expanding American customer base.

Brant Sevensma and WBE continued their partnership until 1922, when WBE bought out his partner. The reasons for the change in ownership are not clear, but it was probably a combination of issues. There were differences in age, in temperament, in attitudes about church unity (Sevensma seems to have been involved in an American Calvinist schism that resulted in the formation of the Protestant Reformed Church), and different ideas about how the business should be developed. WBE had found it difficult to work with his brothers in the family business in Bolsward, and he had not been able to work smoothly with his brother-in-law, Herman Hamstra, in the import business. It could well be that, after eleven years with Sevensma, his restless spirit was simply too large for the partnership.

The last public mention of the Eerdmans-Sevensma company comes in the pages of the *Grand Rapids Press*. On Wednesday, August 9, 1922, in an article headed "Two More Aspire to Legislature," the *Press* announced that "William B. Eerdmans of the Eerdmans-Sevensma Co., book dealers at 207 Pearl-st., is circulating petitions and will be a candidate." It further notes that "[h]e is widely known in the city."

**Grand Rapids Press article, 1922, announcing
WBE's bid to enter state politics**

Nothing more is known about WBE's candidacy for public office, except that it was not successful. He did, however, buy out the interest of Brant Sevensma in the bookselling and publishing business. After 1922 the company's publications bear the imprint of just one name: William B. Eerdmans.

William Bernardus Eerdmans, ca. 1923

The Prosperous Twenties

———

B y the early 1920s, with a wife and two children, a religious publishing company that he now owned by himself, and a prosperous import business on the side, WBE might have imagined that he
had arrived. His offices and warehouse were located at 234 Pearl
Street, in a building he had purchased directly across the street from
the Pantlind Hotel (now the Amway Grand Plaza Hotel) in the heart
of Grand Rapids. In 1923 his son, William B. Eerdmans Jr., was born,
expanding the family yet again.

The building at 234 Pearl Street was a four-story structure somewhat along the lines of the architecture one would see in a Dutch city
— four stories with a narrow front, only about thirty feet wide. On
the ground floor was the bookstore. As you walked into the building,
there was an arcade before you got to the door of the bookstore. On
two sides of the arcade were shelves built into the wall, where an employee would set out books every morning. So when people walked
by and looked into the arcade, they would see bookshelves built into
the walls; and if they were curious at all, they could come in and examine those books, and then perhaps be seduced into walking into
the bookstore itself. It was quite a large retail space, and it had in its
inventory books from many different publishers, just as the Eerdmans bookstore of today does.

The books WBE himself published in the early years of the 1920s
were increasingly written in the English language. American trans-

**The William B. Eerdmans Publishing Company building
at 234 Pearl Street, Grand Rapids, Michigan**

lations of many books by Abraham Kuyper set the intellectual tone. There were also dozens of theological polemics, written by members of one or another faction in the denominational wars that sometimes raged in the immigrant community. For example, WBE became a good friend of the Reverend Herman Hoeksema, a fiery Christian Reformed preacher. During World War I, while serving as a pastor in Holland, Michigan, Hoeksema had gained notoriety for his refusal to display an American flag in his church. "We do not worship a flag or a nation," he declared. "We worship the Lord of all nations." Someone threatened Hoeksema's life for this supposed lack of patriotism, so the latter took to packing a pistol on his way to and from his preaching duties at worship services.

In 1924, Hoeksema was suspended and deposed from his position as pastor of the Eastern Avenue Christian Reformed Church in

The general view of our store presented above gives an excellent impression of the first floor as it appears from the street entrance.

No pains have been spared to make the surroundings and appointments such that they lend charm and atmosphere to the volumes housed within its walls.

Bookstore interior, ca. 1930

Grand Rapids. He was strongly opposed to the "Articles of Common Grace" that the Christian Reformed Church had adopted in its synod that year. Hoeksema was instrumental in founding the Protestant Reformed Church the following year, and he served as its theological lodestar until his death forty years later.

By this time, WBE was convinced that splits and schismatic breakups in the Christian church were not good. He wished to see more unity, not increasing hostility, among fellow believers. But he also believed in the right of people to express — and publish — their opinions freely. Therefore, while he was not sympathetic to the further splintering of Calvinism in America, WBE remained a close friend of Hoeksema and gave him a platform: he published virtually everything this feisty, charismatic leader wrote. He published Hoeksema's polemics early in his publishing company's history, and by the late 1940s, Eerdmans had sixteen Hoeksema titles in print, including a series of commentaries on the Heidelberg Catechism. Hoeksema was a physically vigorous man and often swam across Reeds Lake in East Grand Rapids as a way to work up an appetite. Many times he would walk from his Franklin Street church to the Schnitzelbank restaurant (a round trip of roughly four miles) to have lunch with WBE.

WBE could see that the immigrant community would soon conduct its daily life entirely in the English language, so he gradually phased out his publications in Dutch, though he continued to offer scholarly works in several languages for theological students at Western Theological Seminary (affiliated with Hope College in Holland, Michigan) and Calvin Seminary in Grand Rapids. More and more, however, he began to think about serving a larger market for religious books, all across America rather than merely in a few small immigrant enclaves of the country.

WBE held to a very inclusive sense of Christianity: he believed that people of faith should strive for as much unity as possible. And as a businessman, he saw the wisdom of appealing to many varieties of religious faith. He appreciated many American revivalists of the period — for example, the showman Billy Sunday — even though his soft-spoken, intellectual approach to the faith was very different from Sunday's flamboyance. WBE believed that God maintained a very large tent for his people. Although he had begun by publishing works written almost exclusively by Calvinists, he eventually broadened his scope to include books by members of an astonishing variety of Christian denominations. As an example of his belief, WBE often expressed the hope that when he got to heaven he would be able to speak with Plato and Socrates as well as Moses and Paul.

European Connections

WBE's nephew Jo Eerdmans (1905-1990), son of his oldest brother, Dirk, also had a career that blossomed in the New World. Jo founded Jaguar Cars North America in New York City, and for many years he played an important role as an importer of luxury automobiles from Europe. Late in his life, Jo wrote a set of reminiscences in which he related his memories of his family and commented on his Uncle Willy's kindness and generosity.

During the First World War, early in 1917, my two older brothers, Ben and Klaas, went to Grand Rapids from the Netherlands via Sweden, Iceland, and Canada. Life at the time was very difficult in Holland, and food was scarce. After the Great War, Uncle Willy employed two sons of my Uncle Matthijs, who also lived in Bolsward. . . . [Jo's Uncle Thijs was the tobacco importer and cigar dealer who had made a fortune and later lost it.]

In 1920, Willy visited his birthplace in Holland with his young wife, Paula. Along came Paula's sister Friedel and her husband, Eugen Forsthoff, from Solingen, Germany. One day the party rented a small steamboat to cruise the Frisian lakes, and they invited relatives and a few friends. There must have been between 30 and 40 people. It was a warm sunny day, and by mid-morning everyone who could swim had taken a dip in the lake.

Just before lunch we steamed through the small village of Woudsend, and Uncle Willy saw that the children were just leaving school. We pulled up at the landing wharf and he talked to the children, about 75 of them, asking them to sing five or six songs for us. He promised to pay each one a "botsie" [a coin worth two and a half cents]. The children began their singing and I was dispatched to the local bank to pick up a hundred botsies. The Junior Choral Society of Woudsend was a great success.

Although the Netherlands was neutral in World War I, it was nonetheless under a kind of siege. England had become a virtual enemy of Holland during the Boer War, when the British had fought savagely against white South African settlers, Afrikaners, most of whom were descended from Dutch Calvinists. Bitter feelings about their treatment — massacres and starvation in Mafeking and other concentration camps — still ran high in the Netherlands, with the result that Britain's enemy in World War I was not necessarily Holland's enemy. In fact, when the war ended, Holland gave asylum to Kaiser Wilhelm, confirming many British, French, and Americans in their notion that the Dutch differed very little from the Germans.

In the early twenties, as he was in the process of taking over the publishing business from his erstwhile partner, WBE continued to travel regularly to postwar Europe. His wife and her extended family were Germans who lived in East Friesland, on the other side of the border. Bill Jr. remembers many things about his German relatives:

> My mother's sister Friedel had married Eugen Forsthoff, who was quite wealthy. Eugen's family was connected to the Henckels cutlery factory, and the couple lived in Solingen, Germany, which was the center of the industry. In 1920, Forsthoff, along with his partner, Paul Giesen, founded a new company that produced high-quality scissors and razors. It was quite a stroke of good fortune for my father that his sister-in-law was married to a guy whose family manufactured cutlery: knives, scissors, and razors were very good commodities to add to his import line of blankets, vases, and books. Later on, these products, including meat cleavers, cigar trimmers, and other Solingen steel items started filling our house the way blankets and vases had. My father's import business was growing, and he was doing quite well.

Gathering the Patrimony

Since the mid-1920s, WBE had heard about an extensive collection of standard religious reference works — biblical commentaries, concordances, encyclopedias, and translations — that had been gathered by the publisher George D. Doran. The Doubleday brothers had joined publishing forces with Doran, but they did not particularly care about this religious line of materials. And so the rights to this extensive body of scholarship, not really glamorous in the eyes of the east coast publishing establishment, got passed around a bit, and discounted, and passed on again. Finally, in 1928, WBE bought all the copyrights, all the printing plates, and all the stock of already printed books, thus assembling a huge collocation of important works that became part of what he came to call "the patrimony." In this way he established a tradition of providing religious scholarship and commentary that was of crucial importance to theological schools, seminaries, ministers, and students of Christianity around the world. Because of his solid grounding in the field, his well-established connections with American and European seminaries, his tireless salesmanship, and his wide-ranging friendships in the publishing industry, his business expanded beyond his wildest dreams. By the end of the decade he was on his way to being a major force in the field of religious publishing — not only in America but around the world.

In early 1929, WBE published a comic novel, an unusual venture for him, given his usual concentration on religiously oriented books. Written by one of his downtown cronies, the attorney Dirk Nieland, *'n Fonnie Bisnis* ("A Funny Business") was composed in Yankee Dutch, an immigrant creole that had been widely spoken throughout West Michigan in the previous decades but was beginning to fade as the English language became more important to the community. Nieland invented his own orthography for this half-breed tongue, so that a good deal of the comedy is provided by the language itself, a clear cultural sign that the Dutch language was dying in America.

The novel is a picaresque, telling a series of apparently moral tales in the words of the narrator, recent immigrant Loe Verlak, "peenter, peeperhenger, en dikkereeter" (painter, paperhanger, and decorator). Verlak imagines himself to be a poet and storyteller of the first rank, and the book that features him sold out quite quickly, going through several printings and a second edition within two years. In fact, it provided entertainment at church picnics and social events in West Michigan and Iowa for several decades. H. L. Mencken, after receiving a copy from the author, wrote Nieland to say that once he figured out the idiosyncrasies of Dutch spelling and usage (Mencken spoke German), he found *'n Fonnie Bisnis* to be the finest and funniest immigrant novel he'd ever read.

The Great Depression

The crash of the stock market in October of 1929 was a shock to WBE, as it was to all of America, but his businesses — books and imports — continued for a while without too many setbacks. He reassured his handful of employees that they would be able to count on their jobs, but that he and they might have to reduce their income until the economy regained its footing. As it turned out, he was able to get through the Depression without laying off any workers. Nevertheless, his life changed.

In a panic about the staggering economy, the U.S. Congress enacted the Smoot-Hawley Tariff Act on June 17, 1930. That notorious act, an attempt to bolster failing American businesses in the wake of the stock market crash, raised taxes on foreign imports to their highest levels in more than a century. It increased duties on virtually all goods arriving at American ports from abroad. On average, rates were tripled: they went from 20 percent to 60 percent of the wholesale value of the goods. Immediate retaliations by America's trading partners reduced U.S imports and exports by more than half.

Suddenly, overnight, everything brought into this country from Europe (except for used books, which were exempt) became prohibitively expensive. Smoot-Hawley probably intensified rather than alleviated the economic difficulties throughout the United States, and it certainly made WBE's life difficult. He was in New York City awaiting a large consignment of goods that were on board a ship in the harbor. He had gone there to secure arrangements for the transfer of his imports overland to Grand Rapids. But the tariff had gone into

Above, Ilse, WBE, Bill, and Paula Eerdmans,
Grandmother Install, Eleanor Eerdmans, ca. 1925;
below, John Hamstra with Ilse, Bill, and Eleanor Eerdmans
in front of the family home, ca. 1929

effect while the ship was at sea. Once he found out how much he would have to pay in duties on these products, he realized that he could not begin to pay the tariffs and still make a profit on the products. He was thus forced to walk away from that shipment — and in effect to walk away from that part of his entrepreneurial life. When he returned home, he told his family how deeply it distressed him: he had to leave his blankets and vases and knives on the ship. One desperate financial act of Congress drove him out of the import business.

The publishing business continued to do quite well despite the economic downturn and the demise of WBE's import business. However, the family suffered an indelible loss later that year.

"I had two sisters," Bill explains, "Ilse and Eleanor: Ilse was four years older than me, and Eleanor was two years older. Eleanor and I had a very close relationship. I was the baby of the family, and she would see that I got dressed and fed properly." His memories of that time are dim, but in the late summer of 1930 he was about to turn seven when nine-year-old Eleanor came down with pneumonia. The medical science of the era was usually able to treat the disease successfully, but her case was too far advanced to respond to treatment, and she died within a very short time. "I don't remember the funeral," says Bill, "but I remember the sadness. I still have her picture, and I look at it longingly from time to time."

In the following months, as the family mourned the loss of Eleanor, WBE placed increasing trust and responsibility in the hands of two nephews, Pat and Bernie Zondervan, who were in his employ by that time.

Developing the List

P rior to the Smoot-Hawley Act of 1930, there appear to have been no yearly announcement catalogs of the Eerdmans list of books, though WBE was clearly quite adept at marketing both his books and his "nonbook products" — the cutlery, blankets, and vases. So one can gather that he must have been good at stimulating word-of-mouth distribution. He also may very well have had print ads in the various church periodicals that were published in both Dutch and English in western Michigan and the Christian Reformed community.

But with his full focus on the publishing business after 1930, catalogs began to appear in print that present the diversity of the Eerdmans full backlist. For example, those published lists of the 1930s (early ones were about the size of religious tracts, except much thicker) boasted the "Eerdmans Dollar Sermon Series," a large number of single-preacher sermon collections that one could obtain for $1.00 each (clothbound). Included were collections of ten or a dozen sermons by such famous preachers as Henry Beets (e.g., his Lenten sermons entitled *Man of Sorrows*), W. E. Biederwolf, H. W. Bieber, Paul Dundore, Robert G. Lee, Albert L. Murray, J. K. Van Baalen, Theodore Walz, the redoubtable B. B. Warfield of Princeton, and the Moody Memorial Church favorite Harry Ironside. In addition to his sermons, W. E. Biederwolf had published over twenty "books" with Eerdmans, most of them 25-cent booklets exposing cults and "isms," such as Christian Science, spiritualism, Mormonism, Russellism, Seventh Day Adventism, and evolutionism.

Theology and Apologetics

At this time, shortly after the decade of the 1920s, when conservatives had bolted from Princeton Seminary and rent asunder the massive Presbyterian Church in the USA, it is not surprising to see the large number of books and booklets exposing the evils of the "isms," especially modernism, paganism, materialism, and, of course, evolutionism. Thus the earliest Eerdmans catalogs also advertised a whole library of books by the Christian apologist Harry Rimmer: only three were actually clothbound, but there were twenty-five "paper bound" booklets for 25 cents each, almost all of them on the debate between Christianity and modern science. (Later, in the early 1940s, Eerdmans was to publish Rimmer's *The Lawsuit Against the Bible,* recounting a trial in which he was a defendant.) There were three books by David Simpson on premillennialism, evolution, and the antichrist, plus J. K. Van Baalen's *Our Birthright and the Mess of Meat,* an early exposé of "Spiritism, Lodgeism, Theosophy, Christian Science, and Modernism" that would presage the publication of his popular book *The Chaos of Cults* in the 1940s. W. H. Rutgers exposed another "ism" in his book *Premillennialism in America,* which was a popular belief within rather than an enemy of American fundamentalism.

By the early 1930s, the Eerdmans catalog could also boast of having eight "immortal works of Dr. Abraham Kuyper." Though six of those eight books were collections of Kuyper's "inspirational meditations," two were important and influential works in theology: the massive *The Work of the Holy Spirit* (660 pages) and *Calvinism,* which was a new edition of the Stone Lectures that Kuyper had delivered at Princeton University in 1898, in which he outlined his famous formulation of Calvinism as a life system not only for religion, but also for politics, science, and art. (In the end, the com-

45

A sampling of the Eerdmans list during the Depression and 1930s:

Theology and Apologetics

Six volumes in apologetics by Harry Rimmer

Five books by Philip Mauro, including *The Gospel of the Kingdom* and *Of Things Which Soon Must Come to Pass* (a standard work on St. John's Apocalypse)

Theodore Graebner, *God and the Cosmos*

Henry Beets, *The Reformed Confession Explained*

Loraine Boettner, *The Reformed Doctrine of Predestination;* also *A Summary of the Gospels*

H. Henry Meeter, *Fundamental Principles of Calvinism*

A. A. Hodge, *Outlines of Theology*

B. B. Warfield, *The Plan of Salvation*

Church History

William Stuart, *A Brief History of the Christian Church*

B. K. Kuiper, *The Church in History*

B. K. Kuiper, *Martin Luther: The Formative Years*

Quirinus Breen, *John Calvin: A Study in French Humanism*

---

pany would have nearly twenty books by Kuyper on its list.) More than a century after he gave his *Lectures on Calvinism* (as the Stone Lectures came to be called), they remain in print — and popular — in 2011. Indeed, in the century since Kuyper's death, his influence and name have not diminished in the least, having gone well beyond the Free University of Amsterdam. "Kuyperianism" remains a potent force in the Dutch Reformed academic community, and certainly at Calvin College and Calvin Theological Seminary. Now a Christian liberal arts college, Kuyper College in Grand Rapids (for-

Biblical Studies and Backgrounds

Alfred Edersheim, *Old Testament Bible History* and *Life and Times of Jesus the Messiah* (2 vols.)

William Hendriksen, *Covenant of Grace* (on the Sermon on the Mount)

Albertus Pieters, *The Ten Tribes in History and Prophecy*

J. B. Tidwell, *The Bible, Book by Book*

Edward J. Young, *Commentary on Genesis* (in the Study Your Bible series)

Henry C. Thiessen, *Introduction to the New Testament*

Commentary Sets and Biblical Reference
(all part of the "patrimony")

Robertson Nicoll, ed., *The Expositor's Bible* (6 vols.); *The Expositor's Greek Testament* (5 vols.); and *The Expositor's Dictionary of Texts* (2 vols.)

James Hastings, *The Speaker's Bible* (clothbound, 27 vols., $2.90 per volume)

Jamieson, Fausset, and Brown, *A Commentary, Critical and Explanatory, on the Whole Bible* (1 vol., 1378 pp., $2.95)

James Smith, *Handfuls on Purpose* (10 vols., $1.50 per volume, $16.50 per set): seed thoughts, illustrations, and practical suggestions for sermons.

MacLaren's Expositions of Holy Scripture

International Standard Bible Encyclopedia (4 vols.)

merly Reformed Bible College), even bears his name, as does the Kuyper Center at Princeton Theological Seminary, which supports intellectual inquiry into Calvinist theology and worldview. Today Eerdmans publishes the serial collections of essays from the Kuyper Center, as well as a couple of books each year about Abraham Kuyper. So the company is still *the* publisher of Kuyper for the English-speaking world.

Eerdmans's magisterial work of Dutch Calvinism in 1930 was the three-volume systematic theology by Louis Berkhof, about which *Christianity Today* (a different periodical from today's magazine of the same name) opined: "It is hardly too much to say that this is the most important work in Systematic Theology from an American source that has appeared in recent years. It would require a small library of ordinary books to cover the subjects treated in these volumes." Among his other books on the Eerdmans list in 1930 was *Manual of Reformed Doctrine,* a more popular exposition of the fundamental doctrines of the church for study groups and the general public (both Berkhof books are also still in print in 2011). Then there was, outside the Dutch Calvinist orbit, the long-lasting *Lectures in Systematic Theology* by Henry C. Thiessen of Wheaton College (still in print in 2011).

Christian Fiction and Children's Books

Dr. Stuart Bergsma, the personal physician to the emperor of Abyssinia, published two books of fiction: *Rainbow Empire* and *Sons of Sheba,* the latter a fictional backstory of the Ethiopian eunuch mentioned in the book of Acts. Dr. Richard Pousma, a physician among the Navajo Indians, compiled their folk stories into a collection entitled *He-Who-Always-Wins. A Modern Prodigal* was a Christian novel that retold the story of the prodigal son; but this time the son loses the faith of his family and home when he goes off to the university. This seems to have been a commonly perceived problem, as evidenced in the plot of another Christian novel, this one by Elizabeth von Maltzahn entitled *Erich Ohlson,* which the original *Christianity Today* called a "powerful" story with a "deeply Christian point of view." Von Maltzahn's protagonist is a young student of divinity who, in his eager search for truth, "discards the faith of his fathers in favor of modernism."

Bertha B. Moore, who was to publish thirty-six works of fiction (mostly for younger readers) with Eerdmans between 1930 and 1952, published *Rock of Decision* early in the company's history. Paul Hutchens, whose later prolific output would include the Sugar Creek Gang books, had by the early 1930s published *This Way Out* and *Romance of Fire*. And there were seven booklets (at 40 cents each) of "inspiring poetic verse" by Annie Johnson Flint.

Catherine Vos's *Child's Story Bible* was already a big seller by the 1930s (and is still in print in 2011). In his eagerness to fulfill all the needs of church, scholar, and Christian layman, WBE printed Bibles (in a variety of fancy or inexpensive formats, genuine leather or leatherette, but always the King James Version); the Heidelberg Catechism; and hymnals for the church bodies he was most familiar with, including the *New Christian Hymnal* and the *Reformed Press Hymnal*.

Finally, one could subscribe to *The Religious Digest,* a monthly magazine published by Eerdmans beginning in 1934, which "brings you comprehensive condensations of the best articles in the field of religious thought and life, reviews of the best books and papers, here and abroad." It was advertised on the back cover of the catalog, available for 25 cents per issue, 3 dollars per year.

Competition within the Community

Early in the twentieth century, WBE's sister Nellie had immigrated to America, married a man named Korperhoek, and moved to South Dakota to live. Some years later she divorced Korperhoek; retaining custody of the children, she moved with them from South Dakota back to Michigan. She then married Louis Zondervan, a farmer who soon adopted Nellie's two sons, Peter and Bernard. Though their last name had been Korperhoek, the new family wished to share the name of the stepfather, Zondervan. Divorce was vanishingly rare in the Dutch immigrant community, as it was throughout America in this era, and people struggled to minimize or hide its effects whenever possible.

As her son Peter (b. 1909), whom everyone called Pat, became a teenager, it was painfully clear that he detested living on the farm in Grandville. He wanted to move into the city and find work there. (Part of Pat's story is told in the Zondervan corporate history, *The House of Zondervan* [Ruark, 2006].) His mother and stepfather, to all appearances, provided a loving home for him, and the family was active in the Christian Reformed Church: in addition to attending services twice on Sunday, they were involved in a multitude of church activities and held daily devotions with every meal in their home. Pat felt strongly about his family's religious faith. But he didn't fit easily on the path they had imagined for his life. He dropped out of high school after tenth grade and spent some time at a local business institute. But he didn't care much for formal education, and went no further with it.

On the farm, while walking behind the plow, Pat thought about another life he might be able to lead. To the gentle rhythm of the plodding horses, Pat composed prayers and sermons, which he then declaimed to the round equine backsides in the solitude of the empty fields. He loved the idea of himself as a preacher, and yet he seemed temperamentally unsuited for the education that an ordained pastor in his Dutch community was required to have: a college education, a firm, basic grounding in Hebrew and Greek, and an extensive academic background in church history and Calvinist theology.

Nellie Eerdmans Zondervan could see that her elder son was unhappy. When he was fifteen years old, she asked her younger brother Willy and her sister-in-law Paula to take Pat into their house — to give him a home in the city. The Eerdmans family at that time already consisted of two daughters, Ilse and Eleanor, and an infant son, William Bernard Jr., who had been born in September 1923. Even so, the couple agreed to take Pat into their home. A year or so after their son was born, young Pat Zondervan, fed up with farm life, came to live with his uncle and aunt and to learn the publishing trade in his uncle's business. Pat lived as a member of the family: he slept in the bed that was to become Bill's when he got a bit older, and he occasionally babysat for the children when WBE and Paula went out for the evening.

WBE also gave Pat a leg up in the publishing and bookselling business. A couple of years earlier, when he had bought out the interest of his partner, Brant Sevensma, the entire weight of his import enterprises had descended on his shoulders. Now, with the business prospering, it must have seemed like a good idea to him to bring someone from the family into it. By the late 1920s, Pat Zondervan had taken on a good deal of responsibility in both bookselling and publishing. And in 1928, Pat's younger brother, Bernie, also came to work for the Eerdmans publishing and bookselling firm, though the latter continued to live with his mother and stepfather in nearby Grandville. Like his older brother, Bernie proved to be a quick study. The presence of these two trusted family members freed up WBE to resume his previous habit of traveling and seeking out opportunities. He did not know about the Zondervan brothers' plans to found a business of their own, nor did he suspect that they were laying the groundwork at his expense.

Enterprise, for WBE, naturally involved sharing ideas and opportunities within the family, but he had no notion of sharing ownership in his company. He had worked many years to put it on firm financial ground, and he was determined to keep control. In the immediate aftermath of the Smoot-Hawley Act, his sense of identity was more firmly than ever tied up with his position as a publisher. The family's sadness over the death of Eleanor in 1930 was emotionally all-encompassing, and the grieving father may have immersed himself in commercial activities in an attempt to rediscover his former life.

Within six months after her passing, WBE had forced himself to resume his peripatetic journeys to Europe, concentrating now on the acquisition of book rights in English, and buying up pastoral libraries in both England and Holland. When twenty-one-year-old Pat Zondervan, the older and more dominant of the brothers, talked with WBE about eventually becoming a partner, the latter brushed him off. He had other things on his mind. To his way of thinking, the Zondervans were mere boys; and he probably imagined that he could take their energy and devotion to his enterprise for granted.

But he was mistaken. Coming home from one of his trips to Europe in 1931, WBE revealed that he had found what he took to be clear evidence of his nephew Pat's dishonesty. He believed that Pat had sold sets of Eerdmans books, and put the proceeds into his own pockets. WBE fired him on the spot. Pat's younger brother, Bernie, continued as an employee for several more months, but it became increasingly clear to WBE that the younger brother, too, was working at cross purposes with his uncle's business, so WBE fired Bernie as well.

The Zondervan brothers had learned their trade well, and in the ensuing years their new enterprise prospered, while often making

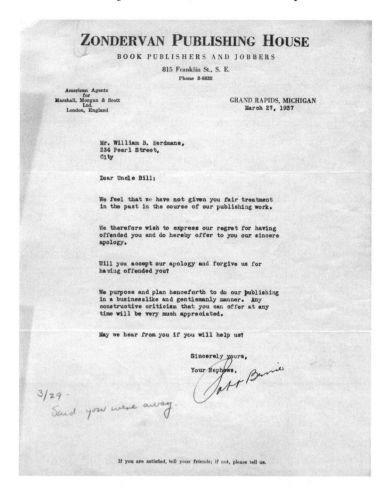

Zondervan brothers' letter of apology

life difficult for their uncle. Within a few years, though, it appears that the Zondervan boys felt a gnawing sense of guilt about what they had done. They were extremely pious; in fact, they had been tempted at times to criticize their uncle for his worldliness. It was certainly true that in certain respects WBE was not a typical member of the Christian Reformed Church, at least of the pietistic strain of Dutch Calvinists. He enjoyed his cigars, and when he ate at the Peninsular Club in downtown Grand Rapids or at the Schnitzelbank on Jefferson Avenue, he enjoyed a glass of whiskey or a manhattan. In fact, that practice had resulted in his church's council receiving an anonymous letter critical of his "public drinking."

On occasion, when he was in Chicago, he would invite people from the Moody Bible Institute to lunch. Despite their abstemiousness, once the era of Prohibition was over, WBE invariably ordered a drink to accompany his food. Although some of the Dutch Calvinist immigrants in West Michigan were pietists and thus teetotalers, he had grown up in Friesland, where teetotalers were rare. He sometimes thought of himself as a cosmopolitan in a narrow world. For his nephews, however, their feelings of spiritual purity involved a strange inversion. They were in some senses more pious than their uncle, yet they were the ones seeking his forgiveness.

In a letter dated March 27, 1937, they sent him an apology, but it was an extremely vague and general one.

Dear Uncle Bill:

We feel that we have not given you fair treatment in the past in the course of our publishing work. We therefore wish to express our regret for having offended you and do hereby offer to you our sincere apology. Will you accept our apology and forgive us for having offended you?

We purpose and plan henceforth to do our publishing in a businesslike and gentlemanly manner. Any constructive criticism that you can offer at any time will be very much appreciated.

May we hear from you if you will help us?

Sincerely yours,
Your nephews,
(signed) Pat and Bernie

There is no indication that WBE responded to this note — either in person or in writing. The feeling of estrangement between the two companies did not diminish. In fact, WBE encountered increasing competition that originated with the Zondervan brothers. They had taken away not only some of his customers but some of his authors, and the two firms regularly engaged in competitive activities. One of those competitions involved the fiery evangelist Billy Sunday (1862-1935), a retired professional baseball player who had become one of the most iconic preachers and revivalists of the early twentieth century. Despite being an ordained Presbyterian, Sunday was not notably Calvinist in his religious views, and his language was often closer to that of a baseball player than a minister. He used words like "jackass" in his sermons and decried "the bastard theory of evolution." However, he was the kind of national figure whose life story would surely sell well.

At one point, shortly after their rupture, WBE and Pat Zondervan found themselves vying for the right to publish Billy Sunday's autobiography. They met with Sunday at his cabin in Winona Lake, Indiana, where he had become the mainstay of the evangelical camp established by the famous evangelist Dwight Moody. Bill Jr. remembers hearing the story from his father.

> Billy Sunday told the two publishers that he would allow one of them to publish his life story, and that he would decide right then and there who it would be. "All you need to do," the evangelist said, "is show me how you pray to God." Then, pointing at my father, he said, "You first."

As a Dutch immigrant and practicing Calvinist, WBE found the idea of competitive prayer a bit much. But, being an entrepreneur and a rising publisher, he gave it his best shot, even though his voice was somewhat tinged with a Dutch accent. In the opposing corner, Pat Zondervan, who eventually became a lay preacher for the Gideon Bible Association, had perfected his prayer technique on the family farm, behind a slow-moving pair of plow horses. He was certainly not intimidated by Billy Sunday's unusual demand. Zondervan's prayer won the day and the book contract. In some ways, this incident came to symbolize a growing difference between the two familial companies.

Dutch and German in America

On several occasions during the 1930s, the Eerdmans family traveled to Europe, visiting relatives in both Holland and Germany while WBE maintained and further developed his relationships with Dutch and British publishers. While in the Netherlands, Bill Jr. lived for several short stints with his uncle Thijs, the tobacconist.

As Bill remembers it, Thijs was an eccentric evangelist at that point in his life. While driving around Bolsward, he'd spot a stranger in another car, get him to stop, roll down his window, and then ask the stranger about the condition of his soul. Despite this religious fervor, Thijs also insisted that he had the right to sell cigars on Sunday, no matter that the laws of the city prohibited it. "If you can catch me," he once told a police officer, "you can fine me."

On these visits, the family would also spend time with Paula Eerdmans's sister and brother-in-law in Solingen, Germany. Bill remembers playfully dueling with his cousin Hans-Günter when they were both teenagers, using real swords that were actually manufactured by the family's factory. Although Bill's uncle Eugen Forsthoff was not a supporter of National Socialism, there were pressures that caused him to send Hans-Günter to a Hitler Jugend camp in the summer.

On one occasion, when he was fourteen or fifteen years old, Bill went with his cousin to the local swimming pool. He remembers being something of a celebrity there because he could swim the Australian crawl, which German children had not generally learned at that point. Hans-Günter later died in combat during World War II — on the Russian front.

"I never saw Hitler," says Bill, "but we'd travel around Germany and there would be a town square projecting his speech on a large screen. He'd fulminate and we'd listen."

**Matthijs Eerdmans's tobacco store in Bolsward,
Friesland, the Netherlands, ca. 1939**

By the late 1930s, as rumors of war increased, WBE did not take his youthful family to Europe anymore, nor did he revisit Germany as often as before. On several occasions he traveled with another Grand Rapids bookseller, Louis Kregel, who had been in business since 1909. The two men would purchase used religious books — biblical encyclopedias and commentaries — at estate sales in the Netherlands and England.

Louis Kregel's nephew Herman Baker had immigrated to Grand Rapids from the Netherlands with his family in 1925, when he was a teenager. Almost immediately Baker went to work selling religious books for his uncle. After years of working for Kregel, Herman Baker decided to strike out on his own in 1939, when he saw the lucrative possibilities in reissuing older, classic religious texts, as Eerdmans had been doing for years. WBE would often visit Baker's bookstore to ask what was selling, with an eye to eventually publishing the most-sought-after books himself. His manner apparently struck

Baker as bordering on arrogance. A year later, in 1940, Baker became a publisher as well as a bookseller. By the late 1940s, a Calvin College student named Nick Wolterstorff was working for Herman Baker as a proofreader when Bill Eerdmans Jr. dropped off some galley proofs for him. It was the first time the two men had met — in what was to become a long and fruitful relationship.

By 1940, as it happens, enterprises that were to become four of the most influential religious publishing houses in America were operating cheek by jowl within the immigrant community of Grand Rapids, Michigan: Eerdmans, Zondervan, Baker, and Kregel. That should not come as much of a surprise. In some ways the Dutch immigrant community, centered in western Michigan, with smaller fraternal enclaves in south Chicago, New Jersey, Iowa, Wisconsin, and the west coast, was a microcosm of American religious life, which has always defied simple explanations. Dutch-Americans were prone to schism and secession, while professing to seek unity in Christ; they had great sympathy for fundamentalism, while they also offered support to elements of the liberal social gospel; they followed charismatic leaders down narrow intellectual and spiritual paths; they indulged in contentious theological discourse that could produce conflict in families and communities; and yet they felt a deep sense of unity beneath all the separatist rhetoric.

They might struggle over how to integrate themselves safely into the vast American society around them, but they always knew they were Americans, not Hollanders. In that respect, too, they were like people all across the country: most Americans had once been immigrants. As the tumult and tragedy of World War II became increasingly part of the national consciousness, other divisions necessarily faded. As immigrants were figuring out how to become part of their new nation, the requirements of war were sure to play a part in the process.

Educating Bill

L ike his two sisters, Bill Jr. attended Christian schools — Baxter and Oakdale — all the way through grammar school and junior high. His father was a supporter of Christian schools as promoted by the Christian Reformed Church, and of the whole concept of Christian education. But WBE also had some ambivalence about being tied so closely to a somewhat narrowly defined Dutch-American culture. And, of course, Mrs. Eerdmans had been raised as a German Lutheran: she spoke no Dutch or Frisian, was occupied with learning English as her children were growing up, and sometimes expressed a certain distaste for the exclusionary tendencies she apprehended in the community.

And so when Bill told his parents he wanted to go to a public school for his high school years, they let him do it. "After junior high was over," says Bill, "I did not want to go to Christian High School because they didn't have a football team."

> I wanted to go to Ottawa Hills High School, where I could play football. I remember one evening after a football game, around twilight, we were all over at the field just hanging around, and someone — somehow or another — had set up a number of card tables on the field. We placed a number of tables end to end, and we young males had started a competition to see who could jump over them. I recall that, after get-

ting a running start, I could jump over three of those card tables. On the football team I played left guard, and I was pretty good on my feet.

Although he enjoyed football, academic life was a different matter. By the end of his first semester of high school, in December 1938, Bill was flunking out. As a consequence, early in 1939, his parents enrolled him at the McCallie School, a Christian military academy in Chattanooga, Tennessee. It was a difficult situation for everyone. In a letter dated February 18, 1939, WBE expressed something of his frustration to the school's associate headmaster, T. E. P. Woods:

> We are getting letters from Billy. "Not so hot." The boy seems to be rather discouraged. Of course, he has only been there a couple of weeks, does not have many friends, and everything is so strange, and we hope that better news will soon come.
>
> As a matter of fact, it stands to reason that "changing horses in midstream" is not always the best thing to do. His intellectual attainments in the Grand Rapids schools were not so good. The boy was always too full of play for that, and really I do not yet know what his capacity is.
>
> I see his predicament, and more or less sympathize with the mess he is in, as he puts it.

WBE makes it clear that he's not primarily interested in intellectual accomplishments for his son. "I myself have been more a student of life than of books," he says. "I want him to get acquainted with a cross section of American life and Christian youth and educators." After further discussion about how he hopes his son will find good things at McCallie, he concludes:

> The boy will have to find his own level and live his own life, whether he be a publisher or a huckster. If he has a cosmopolitan spirit, and has learned to handle men; has learned to be-

come independent and to take initiative; and has acquired a fine sympathetic and Christian attitude toward people and problems: those are the things and the values I crave for him.

WBE concludes his letter by asking, "Have I bothered you too much? If so, forgive me, and lay it to the compassion a father has for his only boy."

Bill had just turned fifteen when he went off to McCallie, and his departure from Grand Rapids began the breakup of all the close associations he'd had with friends in the neighborhood, church, and school — because he was gone for most of his high school years. However, during the next three years, despite occasional problems, he became a solid member of his class at McCallie. Both his father and his teachers noticed that he could be brilliantly insightful at times, but that he was easily bored by the mundane requirements of the classroom and often at odds with the school's rigid sense of discipline. He remembers the experience with a mixture of pride and distaste:

The first year, I was the only Yankee in this Southern school. All I had to do was open my mouth, and people would laugh at me. It was simply that I didn't talk like they did. When I first got down there, I simply did not understand what the guys from South Carolina were saying whatsoever. There were different degrees of the Southern dialect, but they [the South Carolinians] seemed to me the least comprehensible. So I'd get laughs — the Yank talk — just by opening my mouth, and I got to thinking I was pretty funny. I seemed to be a lightning rod for jokes, whether verbal or practical.

One time I fell asleep in history class while we were studying the Civil War. The teacher, who was also the football coach, came over to where I was dozing and said, "Eerdmans! Eerdmans! The Rebs are comin'." And the class of course would roar. There seemed to be a lot of that kind of thing going on.

[McCallie] was military in the sense that we wore uniforms and paraded around with guns (though we didn't shoot them). It was not run by a religious denomination, but was strongly influenced by religion, of a Presbyterian kind, because the headmasters were Presbyterians. We had chapel, and we had to go to church on Sundays — though it could be a church of our choosing.

There was a big annual full-dress parade that we had to attend. It was quite a shindig, the parade of the year, with many of the parents in attendance. The school also had a huge swimming pool (so big it was called "The Lake" by the students). One year I was down by "The Lake" sunning myself, and I decided I would skip the parade. Of course, my absence was eventually noticed. In chapel, before the whole student body, I was forthrightly criticized for my malefaction. Everything you did or didn't do there, you had to submit a note explaining your sins of omission and commission. So I turned in a note about my absence for the big parade, explaining that I was too weak from the effects of the sun. "The sun had sapped my strength" were, I believe, the words I used. The guy who was in charge of the military side of everything — they called him "Colonel Something-or-other" — read this aloud to other students: "Now hear this, this is the most sorry-ass excuse that I've ever heard around here." I suppose they wanted to make an example of me.

I was quite an upstart for practically the whole three and a half years, and there were far too many reasons that eventually got me kicked out of McCallie, after three and a half years, just two weeks before graduation.

One reason was a haircut and a beer. I had gone to the little community of Brainerd for a haircut, and on the way back I stopped at this restaurant that I had become accustomed to stop at and have a beer. I was in my uniform, and I obviously couldn't have a beer in the restaurant with my school uniform in full view. So I'd march back into the kitchen and sit there to be served. At my age, the restaurant guy shouldn't have been serving me beer, but I was a regular customer. This was after school hours, getting on toward supper, so I had to get back for supper. So I was in the dining hall, sitting at my usual place among the round tables — acting rather suspiciously — and one of the headmasters came over and leaned against the wall near our table and just kept looking at me. I did my best to ignore him and act normal, until finally he had convinced himself that something was wrong — so he asked me to get up, and he checked me out and discovered what I had been up to. That, along with all the other infractions, led to my being kicked out.

Bill was allowed to take his final exams at a nearby Seventh Day Adventist college, but he was given a certificate rather than a diploma, and was told he would never be allowed the privilege of graduating from the McCallie School. It was a hard blow for Bill, and perhaps even harder for his father, who drove the long road back to Michigan in stony silence, now and then staring balefully at his abashed son.

Years later, the McCallie class of 1942 held regular reunions. At one of these events Bill, freshly returned from a scholarly seminar in Israel, was chatting excitedly about his experiences there, about his visit to the Holy Sepulchre, and about the many other religious sites he had visited. Someone at the reunion suggested that Bill give the customary invocation.

Immediately someone else stood up and complained, "Why Eerd? He was the biggest sinner we had."

With a smile, Bill replied by recalling the words of Paul, who described himself as the chief of sinners: "Maybe we should all think of ourselves that way."

The War

It was not long after the Japanese attack on Pearl Harbor that Bill Jr., visiting his family in Grand Rapids, expressed his determination to get involved in what had now become America's war. His mother, Paula, was worried to distraction about his impending military service. His life would certainly be in danger, which was, of course, her greatest concern. But behind that fear lay several other intractable sources of anguish. The European war was in its third year, and her suffering German family had been riven by it. One of her nephews, Hans-Günter, the former Hitler Jugend member, was now fighting for the Wehrmacht, and for all she knew, he might end up in the gunsights of her only son, his American cousin. On the other side of the German political spectrum, one of her sisters had married a Jewish man; the two of them had lived in Leipzig and had lost their lives in an Allied bombing raid early on. She felt torn apart by this horrifying conflict. She had hoped that Bill might stay safely in school for a while longer, that he might somehow avoid a direct engagement with its deadly uncertainties.

But her fears were no deterrent to her son. A few months after finishing high school, he enlisted in the army, joining the 36th Infantry Division (the so-called Texas Division). As far as he knew, he was the only non-Texan in the division. "Apparently they needed to fill one more slot," he says. The enlistees trained at Camp Blanding, Florida, and then at Camp Edwards, Massachusetts. On April 2,

Bill Jr. in his McCallie uniform

1943, they shipped out for North Africa. Their convoy landed in Casablanca on April 13, and as Bill remembers the experience, those early weeks seemed almost like a lark. They knew they were at war, of course, but in North Africa the troops might have imagined themselves to be unbeatable. The Americans had recently won a decisive victory at sea in the Battle of Casablanca, and Field Marshal Rommel was having a hard time of it farther to the east. The British victory under General Montgomery at El Alamein in November 1942 had undermined the Axis powers' position in Africa, and opened a wedge for the Allies.

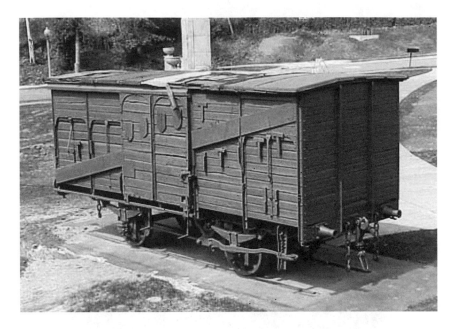

Forty & eight boxcar used for troop transport in North Africa

In an atmosphere that seemed almost festive, the men of the 36th packed themselves into "forty & eights," stubby-looking French railroad cars left over from World War I. The cars had been designed early in the twentieth century to hold forty men and eight horses, which was how they got their name. Now they were loaded with Americans, mostly Texans, as they began rumbling across the northern coastline of Africa from Casablanca to Tunisia.

"We stopped in almost every town," Bill recalls, "making deals with the Arabs who came to the train to sell or exchange things. We were peddling a lot of government-issue material." As an example, every man had been provided with an elaborate receptacle sleeping bag, one part of which was supposed to be stuffed with grass or hay to make sleeping more comfortable. But if you cut off that "litter bag," you could sell it for as much as sixty dollars. "It became a sort of bazaar," says Bill, "with all the trains coming through. The Americans would barter. They'd agree on a price only as the train got ready to leave, and as it was pulling away some GI's would grab both the money and the sleeping bag.

"That meant the next train would have trouble. Word got around pretty fast. If you were in the train right behind some dishonest GI's, you'd find yourself buying a bottle of white wine that turned out to be urine. But you didn't know that until the train was moving."

In September 1943 the African campaign finally concluded with an Allied victory, and Bill was on his way northward across the Mediterranean toward Italy. The 36th Infantry was the first American division to land in Europe, and it would eventually march all the way to Rome and beyond. First, though, the Americans had to establish a beachhead, and the invasion of Salerno began on September 9. Hoping to surprise the German troops, the Americans had planned the assault as a naked landing from the sea. There had been no preliminary bombardment to soften up the enemy, no naval attack to instill fear in the beach's defenders and demonstrate long-range artillery. And, unfortunately, there was no surprise: as the men of the 36th marched ashore from their amphibious troop carriers, they were greeted by an announcement in English over a powerful loudspeaker: "Come in and giff up. Ve haff you covered." Although they were unnerved, the Allies continued their attack, and after intense fighting, managed to secure the beach.

For the next five or six days the combat continued, with the Germans mounting several counterattacks. Buttressed by air support and naval assistance, however, the Allies held the beachhead. Bill remembers one of the assaults:

> We went in — I looked back and a Navy guy who had been next to me was dead in the water. We rushed onto the beach. The two German machine gunners still on the beach were the rear guard of their company. They could see a huge armada in the water, and the air support kept coming. After the initial attack, the Germans got scared and gave up. The two remaining gunners came running and stumbling down the

hill calling, "Nicht schiessen, nicht schiessen." They could see they had no chance. With their little gunners' waistcoats, I thought they looked like Charlie Chaplin. We took them in and went on.

Bill's division was involved in more or less continuous combat for more than a month, occasionally getting a brief break from the action. He did not write home very much during that period, and his parents and Ilse, glued to news reports about Allied actions, worried greatly about his safety. In October 1943 his father received two letters from the McCallie School. The first was from the headmaster, Dr. J. P. McCallie, and began bluntly:

Dear Mr. Eerdmans:

We would like for you to confirm the rumor that has come to us that Bill has been missing in North Africa for some time. We were desperately sorry to hear it. If it is true, Bill is the thirteenth boy in the McCallie battalion that has given his life for his country in this great conflict. Our hearts go out in sympathy to you and Mrs. Eerdmans, but we believe he has not made this sacrifice in vain.

McCallie goes on to ask for a photo to be placed on the wall of the library, and expresses his belief that if Bill has indeed given his life for his country, "he is now with the Lord." A second letter, this one from the associate headmaster, is far more personal:

My dear William,

Yesterday Dr. McCallie showed me a letter from one of our old boys in which he said that he had heard that Bill had been killed in action. I hope that this is not true. During the summer, in fact just the last of June, I received a nice letter from Bill written at Tunisia, telling me about his experiences and his duties. I answered it immediately and have wondered about not getting a reply. But as the Sicilian campaign started soon after, I have supposed he was too busy to write. Please let me know about him, for I am deeply interested and want to share with you whatever has happened — good or bad.

Bill's letter was so cheerful that I can't think of anything but his taking his part and doing it well.

I can't write of anything else now, for my mind and heart are so troubled at hearing what I pray may only be a false rumor.

Love to all of you,

T. E. P. Woods

For several weeks after the arrival of these letters, the family heard no word from Bill. His mother went into mourning, not leaving the house for days on end. Finally, just before Thanksgiving of 1943, a letter showed up in their mailbox. Bill was okay, and he had no idea why one of his classmates might have thought him dead. He promised to write more often so that they wouldn't have to worry needlessly. He probably didn't know — and certainly did not tell his family — that on November 15, the 36th would return to combat after a brief R and R.

From then on, Bill's unit was involved in constant skirmishes and battles throughout the hard winter months. By January 1944, the 36th Division found itself, with other Allied troops, surrounding Monte Cassino in what turned out to be the deadliest battle the Allies had fought up to that point. The Germans had for some time occupied the mountaintop around and beneath a heavily fortified stone monastery, founded in 524 by Benedict of Nursia. Although they were not initially in the abbey itself, their positions were virtually impregnable, so the battle seemed endless.

In February 1944, Bill was severely wounded at Monte Cassino. He did not know for sure whether the shrapnel that sprayed him from head to hip was Allied or German, but his injuries were extensive. He was taken from a field clinic to the large Allied hospital in Naples, where he spent a month being operated on and recovering his strength.

One of his more dramatic memories of the hospital in Naples

The McCallie School
Missionary Ridge
Chattanooga, Tennessee

October 23, 1943

Mr. W. B. Eerdmans
725 Benjamin Avenue, S. E.
Grand Rapids, Michigan

Dear Mr. Eerdmans:

We would like for you to confirm the rumor that has
come to us that Bill has been missing in North Africa
for some time. We were desperately sorry to hear it;
and as it came to us from another boy who heard it
from still another student, we would like to have con-
firmation of it.

If this is true, Bill is the thirteenth boy in The
McCallie battalion that has given his life for his
country during this great conflict. Our hearts go
out in sympathy to you and Mrs. Eerdmans, but we
believe he has not made this sacrifice in vain. It
is for the church, for liberty, for conscience, for
the freedom of the whole world--not only of America--
and we shall never cease to honor his memory in this
school. We have a service flag up now with twelve
gold stars on it out of the 900 or more boys from
McCallie School who are in the service of their country.

Dr. Woods and I would like very much to have a word
from you about the matter as far as you know. We are
gathering pictures of our boys, of a size about 5 x 8,
to place here in an honor album or on the wall of our
library, dedicated to the memory of those McCallie
boys who gave their all for their country and their
God. We believe Bill had the substance of the matter
in him, and that he would now be with the Lord if it
is true that he has been taken away from the earth.
Let us hear from you, please.

Sincerely, your friend,

J. P. McCallie,
Headmaster.

P.S. We hope you
can furnish us
with a recent pic-
ture of Bill.
JFM:V

**The letter sent out by the McCallie School informing the
Eerdmans family of the rumor of Bill's death in combat**

involved a soldier in the bed next to him, a man who suffered from
a significant case of genital elephantiasis. Medical personnel from
all over the hospital — doctors and nurses, orderlies and officers
— came in to examine this unfortunate GI. Some of their interest
was surely medical, although Pfc. Eerdmans thought he detected a
certain amount of prurience as well. Despite the fact that Bill was

recovering nicely, he felt vaguely neglected next to such a medical celebrity.

While he was in the hospital, Bill had occasion to read *A Leatherneck Looks at Life,* by Cornelius Vanderbreggen, a Dutch-American second lieutenant in the Marine Corps. Still a committed publisher's son despite his immersion in the war, he wrote to his father about "this wonderful book."

> The underlying theme is Vanderbreggen's search for a real, assuring, everlasting peace, which he finally finds in Jesus. He gives a vivid picture of Holland — even of Friesland, the province where you were cradled . . . and talks about the country's history. . . .
>
> But what am I telling you all this for, Dad, an old Dutchman like you! All in all, Dad, I think it is a wonderful book, and I would like to know what you think of it.
>
> Your loving son,
> *Bill*

Eager to support his son, WBE arranged to bring out a trade edition of the book, which he published in 1944. Bill Jr. later developed reservations about the jingoistic, gung-ho way that Vanderbreggen characterized the Christian faith. As a footnote, a few years after the war was over, Cornelius Vanderbreggen became an early mentor to the evangelist Pat Robertson, who was, like Bill, an alumnus of the McCallie School.

When Bill finally returned to action, his company had not moved from its position of a month before. It still occupied the same terrain, and so did the Germans. It would take four months, and the Allies would incur nearly 100,000 casualties, before the road to Rome was open and secure.

By late May 1944, with the campaign for Rome still at white heat, Bill and his company stormed the beachhead at Anzio. His company captured Velletri on June 1 and entered Rome victoriously on June 5,

1944. Bill remembers the celebration vividly. At one point, with a big cigar in his mouth, he affected a swaggering pose in the back of a Jeep, impersonating Mussolini in front of one of the former dictator's Roman residences. As he recalls, he got a lot of laughs from a sizable crowd. At least for a short while, it must have felt as though the war had been won.

A few weeks later, in a letter dated June 17, 1944, he wrote a message that showed high spirits and even a certain callousness about the death and destruction all around him. A few Grand Rapids friends had come to Italy, and Bill may have had the idea that the worst of the war was now behind him.

> *Dear Folks,*
>
> "Rangy Rip" says it's the 17th of the month — now I don't know — we'll leave it at that. So Rhinedale the Rooker is in Italy. I would like to meet up with him — tho' more than likely we won't — I'm on the lines most or all of the time. John Pool, Miriam's Wonder of the Ages, is over here too — received a letter from him — he's in the medico detachment of the infantry of the 88th division, & what with Balls [John Ball, a boyhood friend] over here — things seem to become more like home every day — tho' I wouldn't take the whole works over here for all the dough in the world — they know where they can shove every inch of it as far as I'm concerned. It's strictly "no buono" — this ink I'm using I picked off a dead jerry this morning. He was making a getaway on a horse, which stepped on one of their own mines — guts laid strewn all over the road — smelled a bit too.
>
> *Love, Bill*

His division got a few breaks from the action now and then, but it kept moving north through Italy, finally being deployed to France, and then working northward into Germany. It was in Germany, just days before the end of the conflict, that Bill and his comrades en-

countered "the most horrible sight my eyes have ever witnessed."
The 36th Division came upon and liberated Kaufering, where two
satellite camps of Dachau were located.

April 29, 1945

Dear Loved Ones,
    Yesterday we overran two German concentration camps
— for POW's and Jews alike. Most of the POW's were Rus-
sians. The Jews — they were no more. Before any troops got
there the krautheads had burned down the camp and here
and there one could see a few charred bodies. However, the
most horrible sight my eyes have ever witnessed was looking
at some 2 or 3 hundred Jews dumped in piles and in rows
some 2 or 3 hundred yards from the camp — all starved to
death. There was no sign of blood, strangling, bullet holes, or
the like — just a couple hundred starved out, emaciated, & I
don't know what else — bodies — nothing but skin and bones
— bones covered merely by a layer of skin — sunken eyes,
chests, drawn-in stomachs that went back to the spine — bodies naked, half stripped — others with striped pajama-like
garments. A little farther down was another pile of Jews —
these were headless, armless, legless — cut in half — beaten
to pulps — probably those of the Jews who offered some resistance or who cried out for mercy — these Jews, these victims
of these heartless Godless German vermin!!
    The German guards are out there now, digging with their
hands, with shovels, stones, anything — holes in which to
bury their Jewish victims. Some French and Russian forced la-
borers — half crazed over the treatment they have been given
in the last five years by their German conquerors — are running around beating the Germans with shovels, with 2 × 4's,
with their fists — all seeking revenge. One hun was hit over
the head with a 2 × 4 by one huge mad Russian. The hun is
now as kaput as his Jewish victims. "As it was in the days of

Noah. . . ." It seems that all around me I see nothing but death, torture, cruelty, & people in love with Hell.

By May 1, 1945, a week before the end of the war, Bill's unit was in Kitzbuhel, Austria, where they were able to capture Field Marshal Gerd von Rundstedt, the commander of all German forces on the Western front. Bill remembers being part of the group that drove von Rundstedt to an airfield where he would make his formal surrender. "If we had known what we later learned about him," he says, "the Field Marshal might not have made it to the airfield in such good shape."

By the end of hostilities, the 36th Texas Infantry Division had seen four hundred days of combat. It had suffered heavy casualties (3,600 deaths and more than 13,000 wounded), and it would become one of the most highly decorated outfits of the war. Its members were awarded fourteen Medals of Honor, eighty Distinguished Service Crosses, more than two thousand Silver Stars, and countless other honors. The United States Memorial Holocaust Museum has also recognized and honored the 36th for its work securing the subcamps of the Dachau concentration camp system.

Bill could not have known it at the time, but by the end of the war, he had also managed to graduate from high school. In a letter dated April 20, 1945, the headmaster of the McCallie School informed WBE of his institutional decision.

The McCallie School
Missionary Ridge
Chattanooga, Tennessee

April 20, 1945

Mr. W. B. Eerdmans
725 Benjamin Avenue, Southeast
Grand Rapids, Michigan

My dear Mr. Eerdmans:

I am sending you by this mail Bill's diploma. I have gone over our records and am having Miss Zella Woods recopy the records, omitting all references to discipline. The record here will show that Bill was a graduate of the class of 1942 and there will be no reference whatsoever to any past action.

Bill writes Dr. McCallie some of the finest letters that I have ever read, and we are indeed proud of Bill. We join with you and Mrs. Eerdmans in thanking God for his wonderful attitude and what he is doing.

With the very highest regards, I remain

Sincerely yours,

S. J. McCallie
Headmaster

SJM:FS

The letter confirming the graduation of Bill Jr. from the
McCallie School at the end of World War II

Postwar Expansion

In the fall of 1945, right after the end of worldwide hostilities, the Eerdmans Company proudly announced its acquisition and occupation of two new buildings on Jefferson Avenue in Grand Rapids. Only months after the end of the war, WBE had realized that the building he occupied on Pearl Street was no longer big enough for the company's requirements. The Bill Pastoor Ford dealership was in the process of moving its headquarters away from Jefferson Avenue and out to the developing 28th Street beltline, so WBE arranged to purchase the dealership's real estate and buildings on Jefferson to serve as warehouse, bookstore, and office space. Eventually, the Eerdmans Printing Company would also occupy a building on Jefferson, filling up most of two city blocks. The structures were not exactly intended for the publishing business, but they were strongly built and allowed plenty of room to grow. At least WBE could be assured that floors intended to support automobiles could easily handle heavy cases of books.

The publishing office, including the "business and editorial phases," with the shipping department in the rear, was just one block south of the printing plant. The latter, as the 1946 catalog announced, "[is] completely equipped with linotype machines, printing presses of various sizes and kinds . . . receives the edited manuscript, prints it, proofreads it and binds it into the finished product."

The composing room on the second floor of the new Eerdmans building on Jefferson Avenue in 1946

The upper two floors of the publishing offices provided storage space for a great number of books. For the time being, the company retained the bookstore on Pearl Street, which WBE had established in 1921, complete with "Christian supplies of all kinds, Bibles, fiction and non-fiction, church and Sunday School supplies." In publicizing its "complete service . . . with the best in the religious field," Eerdmans said that the publishing company

> was built up with the basic belief that all Christian people, at least of the evangelical persuasion, have sufficient unanimity in teachings and major issues, that they can lay aside controversial questions and emphasize their points of agreement. The Eerdmans policy is to have authors bring out positive and constructive elements of Christian life and doctrine in their manuscripts and to relegate negative and controversial issues to their Synods and conferences. In this way our concern has

**An Eerdmans promotional brochure from the 1940s touted
the "modern sewing machine used in making the quality
binding so characteristic of all Eerdmans books."**

succeeded in bringing together some fifty different denominations and religious groups on our list of authors. The company has thus exercised a unifying influence in the field of
Christian literature. We stand for the genuine gospel of our
Lord and Savior, Jesus Christ, the necessity of regeneration,
with Christian living and works as the expression of the in-
dwelling Spirit, and in gratitude for salvation.

From a small concern, the Eerdmans Publishing Com-

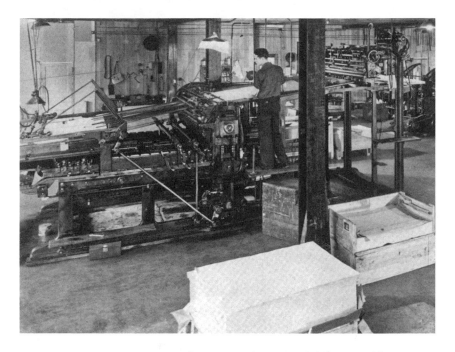

**A press operator runs signatures through a folding machine
in the new printing plant on Jefferson Avenue.**

pany has grown till it now turns out over a hundred titles per
year. We have everything requisite to the production of the
complete book from author to trade. In the days of the great
depression, when so many concerns closed down, the company weathered the financial storms by the united effort and
sacrifice of both publisher and employees. This was possible
through devotion to the cause for which the company stands.
Each employee feels himself a part of a growing organization
which serves the public; and has been instrumental through
the printed page in bringing the everlasting truths of the gospel to great numbers of people in fiction and non-fiction.

It is our aim to make a book not only interesting, but as
scholarly as we can with the material sent in, without changing the spirit, idea, and intent of the author, whose originality

and individuality must ever be zealously guarded. From the smallest juvenile to the most scholarly theological volume, care is given to present the best within our powers with the material available at this time. Close cooperation between our personnel and the author brings satisfaction to all. This cooperation we endeavor to maintain in the publication of each book.

Throughout the entire English-speaking world, Eerdmans books have become known and won recognition for high standards of quality. Furthermore, our world-wide connections put us in an advantageous position to sell and promote books and bring them to the attention of editors of the leading periodicals for review.

The first postwar catalog was a hefty sixty-four-page bulletin that devoted its first twenty-four pages to adult and juvenile Christian fiction and children's Bible stories, followed by the many sets and series, books on church history and biographies of the Reformers, a grouping called "Home Devotional Library," biblical study aids and sermons helps, and, finally, the most scholarly books of theology. The catalog amounted to an inventory of the entire Eerdmans backlist, with a back inside-cover-page listing of "publications just released" and "forthcoming publications." The fat new catalog's back cover — as well as a four-page inset on glossy paper — celebrated *The Religious Digest,* which each month reviewed the "finest in current literature."

WBE was in a mood to celebrate world peace in 1945, including the almost miraculous return from combat of his only son, his successor. His company was coming out of World War II with a big splash — both in new facilities and a very large list of new books along with the backlist titles — and heading into an optimistic future of discovery and expansion.

The Zondervan Affair Redux

By the end of 1945, as troops were still returning from the farther reaches of the war effort, the American economy was preparing for a boom that would last for decades. Returning soldiers married and began raising families in a new era of peace and prosperity. Three days after Christmas, on December 28, 1945, WBE received a second letter from his nephews Pat and Bernie, eight years after their first apology. But this letter was not addressed to "Uncle Bill," as their previous one had been. In fact, the letter spelled his name wrong at every occasion. "Dear Mr. Eerdman [*sic*]:" it began. There followed an invitation to the LaSalle Hotel in Chicago, where a meeting was being arranged "for the purpose of ironing out some difficulties which have been brought to our attention." The invitation was also extended to Stuart Anderson, "the business manager of Eerdman's [*sic*] and Mr. W. Barbour of the F. H. Revell company" in New York City.

The Zondervans had arranged for three prominent fundamentalists to serve as impartial "judges" at this meeting: Will H. Houghton, the head of the Moody Bible Institute in Chicago; J. Palmer Muntz, the director of the Winona Lake Assembly and also the founder of Youth For Christ International; and E. Schuyler English, a prominent fundamentalist scholar and writer.

The Zondervans agreed to pay all expenses for the participants, and they even went so far as to enclose a self-addressed stamped envelope. The envelope was never used. No one from Revell or Eerdmans attended this meeting, which may well have looked to them like an attempted whitewash. People who might have accused the Zondervans of professional misbehavior were being invited, and an elaborate defense might well have been mounted against all comers.

No matter what the rationale, WBE was clearly determined not to participate in accusing his nephews publicly. He had never publicly aired his grievances against them, though he remained convinced of their perfidy. He was pained by the very idea of leveling accusations against members of his own family. And yet rumors swirled throughout the business. Those rumors, plus a gnawing

ZONDERVAN
PUBLISHING
+ HOUSE +

TELEPHONE 81.438 · · 847 OTTAWA AVENUE, N. W.

GRAND RAPIDS 2, MICH.

December 28, 1945

Mr. W. B. Eerdman
W. B. Eerdman Publishing Co.
234 Pearl Street
Grand Rapids, Michigan

Dear Mr. Eerdman:

Kindly accept our invitation to attend a special meeting at the LaSalle Hotel, Chicago, Illinois, May 13th or 14th, for the purpose of ironing out some difficulties which have been brought to our attention. We feel that to clear the atmosphere, a meeting such as this would prove of mutual benefit.

This invitation is going likewise to:

Mr. Stuart Anderson
W. B. Eerdman's Publishing Co.
Grand Rapids, Michigan

Mr. W. Barbour
C/o F. H. Revell Co.
158 Fifth Avenue
New York City, New York

Dr. Will H. Houghton, Dr. E. Schuyler English and Dr. J. Palmer Muntz have consented to serve as impartial "judges" at this special meeting. If you wish, you may also invite three or four additional gentlemen to sit in on this special conference as impartial "judges".

We trust that this suggested plan will be the step necessary to bring us into a good relationship which will be conducive to a

"Distinctive Religious Books"

Zondervan "hearing" letter, p. 1

Mr. W. B. Eerdman
December 28, 1945
Page 2

spirit of good-will and cooperation between us.

      We will pay all expenses, traveling, hotel room, etc.

      Enclosed you will find a self-addressed, stamped envelope
for your convenience in replying.

Sincerely yours,

ZONDERVAN PUBLISHING HOUSE

P. J. Zondervan, Partner

B. D. Zondervan, Partner

PJZ/iw

Zondervan "hearing" letter, p. 2

Chicago, Illinois
July 22, 1946

Mr. Wm. B. Eerdmans
Wm. B. Eerdmans Publishing Co.
234 Pearl Street, N. W.
Grand Rapids 2, Michigan

Dear Mr. Eerdmans:

On May 14, 1946, by invitation of the Zondervan Publishing House, the undersigned met at the La Salle Hotel, Chicago, with the following representatives of that organization: P. J. Zondervan, B. D. Zondervan, T. W. Engstrom, and Al Ramquist.

The purpose of the meeting was to hear and adjudicate informally some of the charges and complaints that have been "going the rounds" in relation to the business ethics and practices of the Zondervan brothers.

We were disappointed that you did not find it convenient to be present at the meeting, for some of the complaints that have come to us and were discussed at the gathering emanated from conversations that you have had with authors and other publishers.

Those who met discussed and delineated, one by one, only the various reports that have come to our ears; that is, to the so-called "judges," or to members of the Zondervan organization. Those complaints ranged from copyright jumping and appropriation of titles to stealing of authors, and included all sorts of charges.

May we say that all the complaints were old? We are not cognizant of any new charges, and those who might have brought them (if there are any) were not present to do so.

The Zondervans gave their versions of each of the complaints in a very frank manner. They admitted having erred in times past, and they also reported adjustments that they had made in respect to certain of these doubtful cases.

There is no profit in recording the proceedings in detail. After thorough analysis and unreserved expressions of opinion concerning the whole situation, the undersigned came to the conclusion that the Zondervan brothers had in times past performed and followed certain practices which we would not deny as having been doubtful and unethical. At the same time the way in which the Zondervans faced the issue was satisfactory to us, and we whole-heartedly believe that the representatives of the Zondervan Publishing House have ceased from such actions and that there will be no repetition of them in the future, and no reason for complaint.

It seemed wisest to us at this time, rather than to prepare an open letter to the interested parties, broadcasting it widely, to send this personal letter to a few of the people most concerned.

We feel sure that you will be interested to learn of the outcome of the meeting, and that with us you will help to put to silence some of the rumors that may arise from time to time.

Faithfully yours,

(Signed)   Will H. Houghton
J. Palmer Muntz
E. Schuyler English

Conclusions of hearing on Zondervan corporate behavior

sense of guilt, were apparently the underlying reasons for the LaSalle Hotel meeting.

The session, played out in front of three prominent church-men, was arranged by and attended by people from the Zondervan organization. No one else from the world of publishing attended. Two months after the meeting, which was held in May 1946, WBE received another letter, this one from the three judges who had presided. In exceedingly careful language, which corporate attorneys had apparently been working over for those two months, the judges describe their hearing and set out their conclusions. No accusations were brought by any outside witnesses, so the charges consisted only of "the various reports that have come to our ears. . . . Those complaints ranged from copyright jumping and appropriation of titles to stealing of authors, and included all sorts of charges."

Then, without exonerating or convicting, the judges interject: "May we say that all the complaints were old? We are not cognizant of any new charges, and those who might have brought them (if there are any) were not present to do so."

After describing the Zondervans' response to these charges (which had, after all, been brought by the selfsame Zondervans), the judges begin to pass judgment. "There is no profit in recording the proceedings in detail," they say, presumably knowing full well that detail is the essence of complex legal matters.

> After thorough analysis and unreserved expressions of opinion concerning the whole situation, the undersigned came to the conclusion that the Zondervan brothers had in times past performed and followed certain practices which we would not deny as having been doubtful and unethical. At the same time the way in which the Zondervans faced the issue was satisfactory to us, and we whole-heartedly believe that the representatives of the Zondervan Publishing House have ceased from such actions and that there will be no repetition of them in the future, and no reason for complaint.

The "proceeding" seems to have concluded with a determination to sweep these old practices under the rug in the interest of the greater good and a bright future. The judges' letter to WBE was found in late 2010, not in the company archives, but stuffed in a Zondervan Christmas catalog that WBE had squirreled away among old receipts and corporate ledgers.

After this proceeding, WBE and his nephews did indeed repair their relationships, at least to the point where they maintained collegial contacts and served on boards together, sharing business opportunities and cooperating in a variety of ways. But Paula Eerdmans was not as sanguine as her husband was. Pat Zondervan had lived in her home as a member of her family — like a son, she had thought. Now, though she wished it were otherwise, she could not get over her feeling about him. Her son, Bill, with his puckish way of expressing complex quandaries, says, "I wonder whether I should forgive my mother for her inability to forgive Pat."

Bill remembers a very touching occasion — an act of grace — that served as a conclusion to the family rupture. It happened years later, in 1988: WBE had been dead for more than twenty years, and his wife had also died. The huge Zondervan publishing conglomerate had been sold to Rupert Murdoch and HarperCollins; Bernie Zondervan had died, and his older brother, Pat, had suffered a debilitating stroke. One day Pat limped into the offices of Eerdmans on Jefferson Avenue. He noticed his cousin, Bill, in his office, but before greeting him, he tipped his hat and stood looking respectfully at the life-sized portrait of WBE that always hung on the wall in the reception area. Then, with a crooked smile, he walked over to Bill and whispered in his ear, "Keep on publishing!" Bill was happy to oblige.

William B. Eerdmans Sr.,
painting by Armand Merizon, 1959

Years of Growth

Expanding Borders

Up until World War II, Eerdmans had been pretty content, in its publishing of theology, with a relatively small stable of Dutch Calvinists, who wrote in both Dutch and English, and with releasing them either in the Dutch original or in English translation for a grateful readership in the Dutch-American community. Some of these WBE acquired on his own, and some he picked up from other publishers (e.g., Abraham Kuyper's *The Work of the Holy Spirit* had first been published in 1900 by Funk and Wagnall's). He also had a connection in Grand Rapids with Calvin College and Seminary, and he published some distinguished professors from those institutions early on, a couple going back to the very earliest publications of the company in the 1910s.

At the same time, however, WBE was closely associated with people from Moody Bible Institute, and for years he served on the board of directors of the Winona Lake Association. Indeed, the fundamentalist and evangelical movements in America had never been very distant from the company, and WBE had participated in the developments in those theological trajectories, which were affecting his own coreligionists and those in the larger Reformed community as well. By the early 1940s, the fundamentalist-modernist rift that had been precipitated by J. Gresham Machen's breaking away from Princeton Seminary and establishing Westminster Seminary in 1929 (and his subsequent ouster from the Presbyterian Church in the USA) was growing more and more contentious. By the end of World War II, the Eerdmans list of titles featured six books by the separatist Machen (1881-1937): *What Is Christianity? What Is Faith? Christianity and Liberalism* (still in print in 2011), *Faith in the Modern World, The Christian View of Man,* and *The Origins of Paul's Religion.* However, as Bill Jr. puts it,

> [u]nder the influence of Harry Emerson Fosdick and others, American mainstream Protestantism became increasingly enamored of modernism. Because of that, ISBE, Jamieson, Fausset, and Brown *(Critical and Experimental Commentary on the Bible),* and other theological classics of the nineteenth century were superseded by a modern crowd of commentators. New York publishers who held those older standard works didn't care to continue selling them. My father picked up many of these books for as little as a nickel a copy from publishers who didn't wish to hang on to them. He also purchased copyrights in those instances where that was a concern. Apparently the New York publishers, including Funk and Wagnall's, Doubleday, and others didn't know (or didn't care) about the strength of the Midwestern market for conservative commentaries.

Already by the late 1940s, however, WBE saw that he had less in common with the separatist-fundamentalist wing (the "come-outers") and more in common with the moderate — and, in his view, the more thoughtful and intellectual — wing of the evangelical movement. One of the biggest developments during that postwar period was the establishment of Fuller Seminary in Pasadena in 1947 (cofounded by the radio evangelist Charles Fuller and Harold Ockenga, the well-known evangelical at the Park Street Congregational Church in Boston, across from the Boston Common). Ockenga popularized the term "new evangelicalism" in the early 1950s, but he might well have used it in reference to Fuller's professors and students at the seminary's inception.

Carl F. H. Henry, one of the charter members of that faculty, convinced Edward John Carnell (a friend who had an educational pedigree very similar to his own — Wheaton, Westminster, ThD from Harvard, and PhD from Boston University) to join the faculty in 1948. As George Marsden tells the story in his book *Reforming Fundamentalism,* Carnell was a brilliant teacher and prodigious writer who, when he was still under thirty, "had worked out his own apologetics in *An Introduction to Christian Apologetics,* which won the much-heralded Eerdmans Evangelical Book Award Competition in 1948," with its prize of $5,000 (a good year's salary at the time).

Carnell, who later served as president of Fuller, received a good deal of attention for his insistence that Christianity offered a philosophically and intellectually coherent view of life. WBE found common cause with those founders and first faculty members of Fuller because, as Marsden points out, he shared their allegiances to:

1. Protestant/Reformation Christianity;
2. the American evangelical heritage; and
3. classical fundamentalism.

Basically, Eerdmans had followed the same trajectory in reforming fundamentalism — that is, finding a "new evangelicalism" — that Fuller did, and this was not the trajectory of Calvin College and Seminary or the Christian Reformed Church. (Although Eerdmans has often been thought of as the publishing arm of Calvin College because the two institutions have lived together in the same city for a century, that has not been true since at least the late 1940s.) Soon WBE's company was publishing books by much of the Fuller faculty, including Henry and Carnell, Everett Harrison, William LaSor, Bela Vassady, and George Eldon Ladd — and many who came after those early faculty stalwarts. It did not hurt Eerdmans's cause that the founders and early professors at Fuller were almost all friends of Billy Graham, and some were quite important to his career. In fact, when Graham's mild ecumenism had made him a target of attacks by the Carl McIntires and Bob Joneses among the separatist fundamentalists, Graham found friendship, support, and solace among his friends at Fuller. Graham's great success, beginning in 1949, had a strong — if usually indirect — impact on Fuller.

At any rate, by the late 1950s, Fuller and the "new evangelicals" had broken with fundamentalism, their cause strengthened in part by the popularity of Graham. And the "new evangelicals" themselves had begun to see the coherence of certain aspects of Kuyperianism with their worldview. Even before he began teaching his first course at Fuller, Carl Henry had published *The Remaking of the Modern Mind* with Eerdmans in 1946. According to Marsden:

> [T]he very idea of remaking a "mind" was a concept that was far more developed in the Dutch Calvinist tradition than elsewhere in American evangelicalism or fundamentalism. . . . What Henry and the new evangelicalism found in Kuyperian thought was a twentieth-century conservative Christian articulation of a point that had been part of the reformist side of the American evangelical heritage but which had diminished severely in fundamentalism since the 1930s. The point was the broadly Calvinistic vision that the Christian's mission involves not only evangelism but also a cultural task, both remaking the mind of an era and transforming society. . . .
>
> The importance of this general vision for fundamentalism became most apparent with the publication in 1947 of Henry's manifesto, *The Uneasy Conscience of Modern Fundamentalism.* The latter book complemented *Remaking of the Modern Mind,* though it was much less elaborate, by presenting the second part of Henry's program — that dealing with social issues. In defining what Christians needed, both Henry and Harold Ockenga, who wrote the introduction, used a phrase that was already a cliché in the Dutch-American com-

munity: a "world-and-life" view. By this they meant that transformation of thought and action should go hand in hand, that Christians should develop a comprehensive worldview that could be applied to all of life, including its social and political dimensions.

The absence of this worldview was what Henry and Ockenga saw as the major weakness of fundamentalism, with its preoccupation with separation from modernism and liberal Christianity.

Later, Carl Henry, who had taken what was supposed to be a one-year leave from Fuller (which turned into twelve years — 1956-68), became the first editor of a reborn *Christianity Today,* founded by Billy Graham. In addition to two more books by Henry *(The Protestant Dilemma* and *The Drift of Western Thought)* by 1952, and two more by E. J. Carnell *(The Theology of Reinhold Niebuhr* and *Television: Servant or Master),* Eerdmans published George Eldon Ladd's *The Blessed Hope, The Gospel of the Kingdom, The Presence of the Future, Commentary on the Revelation of John,* and his enormous — and enormously influential — *Theology of the New Testament* (all Ladd titles are still in print in 2011). By the early 1950s, Eerdmans was publishing those who were moving from fundamentalism to the new evangelicalism, mostly at Fuller Seminary; but those authors included scholars who were working elsewhere as well, including Carnell's good friend Bernard Ramm at Baylor University (*The Christian View of Science and Scripture* [1954] and later *The Witness of the Spirit* [1959]), Gordon Clark, and Vernon Grounds.

By 1957, Carl Henry had completely distanced himself from Carl McIntire, Bob Jones, and the fundamentalist separatists when he said, "The real bankruptcy of fundamentalism has resulted from a harsh temperament, a spirit of lovelessness and strife." By that time, those at Fuller held the ideal of going back to a prefundamentalist era, when evangelicals combined substantial scholarship with a fervor for action. As Marsden expresses it, "Nowhere did this have greater appeal than at Fuller." Except for Charles Woodbridge, who left Fuller about then, all the Fuller professors sided with Billy Graham against the separatists and militant dispensationalists.

Although WBE certainly sympathized with the moderate and more ecumenical "new evangelicals," his company continued to keep in print at least six books by the key figure in the antimodernist movement, J. Gresham Machen, as well as a thick biography of Machen by Ned Stonehouse, and a book entitled *The Infallible Word* by the Westminster Theological Seminary faculty, not to mention earlier books by B. B. Warfield and Charles Hodge.

International Connections

During this resurgence, Eerdmans also became the American religious publisher with the most European contacts. Editor-in-chief Jon Pott puts it this way:

> In many ways, Eerdmans has long felt close to its English, Dutch, and Scottish counterparts in publishing. The roots of the company are, after all, ultimately not in the American fundamentalist/evangelical movement and combat, whatever the many connections with the latter have been. WBE's feeling of continued closeness to his Dutch roots meant that he often tried to feed Dutch theological, sociological, and political materials to an American audience, and a strong connection with Europe, both the Continent and the United Kingdom, continues at Eerdmans to this day.

Inter-Varsity and Paternoster Presses in the UK

Eerdmans was close, in its British relationships, to both the traditionally evangelical Inter-Varsity Press (IVP) and its director, Ronald Inchley, and Paternoster Press (coming out of the Plymouth Brethren tradition) and its publisher, B. Howard Mudditt. WBE had established an initial relationship with Inchley, and Bill Jr. later became very close to Inchley for many years. "He was a fine Christian publisher," says Bill, "a model for me. After his death, I gave a talk at IVP, emphasizing how much I admired him, both personally and professionally. After Inchley, we had a long and warm relationship with Frank Entwistle, who has now been succeeded by Brian Wilson." With IVP, Eerdmans published such books as the Tyndale Commentaries, John Stott's *Basic Christianity,* and J. I. Packer's *"Fundamentalism" and the Word of God,* the latter two of which are still on the Eerdmans list. And with Paternoster, where Howard Mudditt was succeeded by his son Jeremy, Eerdmans has published, among many other projects, the New International Greek Text Commentary, coedited by I. Howard Marshall, W. Ward Gasque, and Donald Hagner. This set includes some of Eerdmans's most significant scholarly commentaries, among them volumes by R. T. France, James D. G. Dunn, Anthony Thiselton, and I. Howard Marshall himself. The Eerdmans in-house editor for that massive project has been the veteran John Simpson.

Bill often went to see both Inchley and Mudditt, and he considered them to be close friends. "I'd buy rights from them, and even though we were technically competitors, we were always cooperative with each other. The great [New Testament] scholar Fred Bruce was important to both of those presses, and of course to us. We enjoyed wonderful relations for many years."

Back in the early 1950s, a number of people in more progressive evangelical circles were getting tired of backward-looking New Testament scholarship. Bruce, with his brilliant commentary on the Greek text of the book of Acts, single-handedly brought a new spirit to evangelical scholarship. It was no longer possible, after Bruce, to go on in the same old ways. When Edmund Wilson wrote a series of articles about the Dead Sea Scrolls for *The New Yorker* magazine, Bill Jr. sent those articles to F. F. Bruce, who wrote a book on the subject (*Second Thoughts on the Dead Sea Scrolls* [1956]). Over the years, in addition to his work as the general editor of the New International Commentary on the New Testament, Bruce published some two

*"We rather fancy this little novel of yours, Brown. Would you
consider one million six up front for it?"*

dozen books with Eerdmans. In that perhaps nobler era, a number
of those books had been published for years before someone noticed that no contract had ever been signed! Bruce, in his memoir, *In
Retrospect,* comments on the warmly collegial spirit he saw among
the Grand Rapids publishers:

> Grand Rapids is best known in the Christian world as the
> home of great publishing houses. I cherish a memory of Mr.
> Eerdmans standing at the entrance to Calvin Christian Re-
> formed Church, Grand Rapids, where I had been preaching
> that Sunday evening, with one of his arms round Herman
> Baker and the other round the late Bernard Zondervan, say-
> ing, "I don't regard these men as *competitors;* I regard them as
> colleagues!" I cherish the memory of Mr. Eerdmans; he

showed me much kindness. "Ask what you will," he said to me in an expansive mood; "the sky's the limit." I took him at his word — almost; I didn't quite ask for the sky.

The one-volume *New Bible Commentary* and the one-volume *New Bible Dictionary,* which were announced on the cover of the 1955 catalog, originated with InterVarsity Fellowship in London. Bill points out:

> We copublished their Tyndale series, so we were aware that IVP worked with all the most accomplished conservative New Testament scholars in Great Britain. They produced the New Bible Commentary and a Bible dictionary, and we copublished them in the U.S. We either gave them a sum of money or a certain number of copies of the book as compensation.
>
> We were the American publishers, but editorially these were IVP products. This relationship lasted for decades — more than thirty years. Then, as our contract with them was expiring, IVP placed these works with their American wing. So we developed our own commentary, with Jimmy Dunn and John Rogerson. We got them to do a new commentary from the ground up. We found that there was a decent market for a one-volume commentary and also for a one-volume dictionary of our own making; we commissioned David Noel Freedman and Astrid Beck to edit that volume.

Eerdmans may have been the first publisher with evangelical connections to go to the Frankfurt Book Fair, where it now has a long history. That book fair is especially important for cementing relationships between and among international publishers. People buy and sell rights to publish in a range of nations and languages; they wine and dine each other; and in some ways the socializing and schmoozing becomes an important part of forging an international identity for them.

Over most of the past three decades Bill and Jon Pott represented the company at the fair. Bill's son Sam also became part of the contingent. A fluent speaker of French, Sam got along well with the company's European counterparts, and he was often involved in one or another new venture. In his role as marketing director, Sam worked with distributors around the world. It was not at all surprising, according to Pott, for Sam to visit a college — Moore College, say, in Australia — and come away not only with the usual book orders, but with a new manuscript or two as well. In Europe, Sam was especially close to English houses such as Canterbury, while also working with French and German houses. His work took him to Asia, especially Korea, as well. He also enjoyed a very close connection with the Canadian publisher Novalis. In recent years, Tom DeVries has joined the action as Eerdmans' first fulltime rights manager.

The visits to Frankfurt included myriad opportunities for the visiting Americans to get lost. The fair was held at the sprawling Frankfurt Messe convention center. For about twenty years, as Pott recalls it, the company rented a car, and whoever drove managed somehow to get lost or diverted. Often enough, they'd leave the Autobahn to exit for the fair, only to inadvertently wind up back on the Autobahn in short order, headed back where they had come from — or worse! Once, in Sachsenhausen, the rental car accidentally ended up going down some tram tracks, having left the paved station platform and now thumping across the railroad ties. Sam checked behind them for oncoming tram traffic and gave instructions to back up to a nearby platform, where they could again regain the road. On one occasion the Eerdmans contingent got so lost that Bill hailed a taxi, which the rental car could then follow to its destination. In its wisdom, the city of Frankfurt finally installed a train station inside the exhibit complex, and things went much more smoothly for the intrepid publishers thereafter.

Despite the occasional misdirection, a host of worthy projects emerged from these meetings. As one prominent example, Eerdmans collaborated with Lion Publishing in the UK in the co-publication of several of what became a successful series of hand-

Jan Kok and Marlin Van Elderen, colleagues at the WCC

books, beginning with the *Lion/Eerdmans Handbook to the Bible.* Enduring and productive friendships began with David and Pat Alexander and with Tony Wales, among others, at Lion.

In addition to the cooperative ventures mentioned above, the company, under the editorial leadership of Jon Pott since 1982, has pursued a host of activities with other international houses whose interests in some ways coincided: the Anglican SPCK; the English Catholic publisher Darton, Longman, and Todd; Mowbray; Lutterworth;

the Scottish press T&T Clark; SCM; Marshall Morgan and Scott; Hodder and Stoughton; Collins, later HarperCollins; Canterbury; and Continuum. The many coeditions with English publishers have included, beyond those noted above and elsewhere, books by successive Archbishops of Canterbury — Michael Ramsey, Robert Runcie, George Carey, and Rowan Williams. The current Archbishop has graced the Eerdmans list with several books, including his masterful study of Arius (Williams is himself a theologian of the first rank) and *Writing in the Dust,* a pastoral reflection written immediately after 9/11, which he lived through himself only a few blocks away. The company also publishes a substantial biography of him by Rupert Shortt, religion editor of the London *Times Literary Supplement.*

Continental collaborations have occurred with Vandenhoeck and Ruprecht, a German academic publisher with a history going back more than 275 years; Mohr Siebeck, another German house; the Swiss firm Theologische Verlag Zürich; and of course, among several other Dutch partners, Kok Publishers of Kampen, which had been one of the inspirations for WBE when he first entered into the publishing business and has remained a particularly close friend and publishing partner over the years since. Such European collaborations have been replicated elsewhere in the world as well — in Africa (especially South Africa), Asia (especially Korea), and South America (especially Brazil).

The Fathers

The writings of the ante-Nicene, Nicene, and post-Nicene church fathers had been edited by Philip Schaff in the nineteenth century and were in the public domain. All three of these series, a classic anthology of patristic works, were in the public domain. Eerdmans published the three sets — "the Fathers," as they were called — for decades, and the company became well known internationally for the quality and reliability of these offerings. A competitor eventually put out a less expensive version of those works. At such low prices, Eerdmans was unable to maintain the quality it wanted, so it finally dropped "the Fathers" altogether.

Commentaries

The New International Commentary on the New Testament (NICNT) was announced in 1946 as a seventeen-volume series. The first volume, *Luke* by Norval Geldenhuys, appeared in 1951, followed by *1 Corinthians* by F. W. Grosheide and *Galatians* by Herman Ridderbos. The NICNT was featured on the cover of the 1956 Eerdmans catalog with Ned Stonehouse as the original general editor of the series. Eerdmans had taken over the volume on Luke, which was already in print from a British press, and Stonehouse took the series from there. After Stonehouse died, F. F. Bruce became the general editor; after Bruce's death in 1990, Gordon Fee took over. "The series is still not quite completed," says Jon Pott, "though we're nearly there, and we continue to replace dated volumes. This past year we replaced our commentary on the Gospel of John with a magnificent new work by Ramsey Michaels, and we also just published a splendid replacement commentary on the book of James by Scot McKnight. We are determined to keep this series current."

The NICNT was joined in due course by its counterpart, the New International Commentary on the Old Testament, the first three volumes, a commentary on Isaiah by E. J. Young, appearing in 1972. Young served as the initial editor for this series, followed by R. K. Harrison, who after a number of years passed the baton to Robert Hubbard, who remains the series editor today, working closely with Allen Myers, the Eerdmans staff editor for the series.

The NICNT was also complemented by the Pillar commentaries, a series that began in 1991 with two independent volumes considered too large for the Tyndale New Testament Commentary, which Eerdmans published at that time. Those first two volumes were D. A. Carson's commentary on the Gospel of John and Leon Morris's on Romans. In 1992, it was decided to make these two volumes the first in the completely new mid-level commentary, the Pillar series, which took its name from the Doré illustration of Greek pillars used on the dust jacket. Milton Essenburg, who had also been the in-house editor for NICNT, commissioned some of the new commentaries for this highly successful series, and D. A. Carson, the outside general editor, commissioned the remainder.

Reference Works

WBE and Calvin Bulthuis, his new editor in the late 1950s, decided to revamp the massive and classic *International Standard Bible Encyclopedia* (*ISBE,* as it has come to be known). Carl F. H. Henry, editor of *Christianity Today,* was the midwife to this new edition by reason of his strong support; and Geoffrey Bromiley, Henry's former colleague at Fuller Seminary, became the editor. Eerdmans' original inside man on the project was John De Hoog, who, when he left the company, was replaced by Edgar Smith, a PhD in New Testament studies. In the end, the process took sixteen years, much longer than Bill had imagined possible.

Perhaps the most important contribution of Eerdmans to biblical and theological publishing in the 1960s and 1970s was the English translation of the nine-volume *Theological Dictionary of the New Testament,* edited by Gerhard Kittel and Gerhard Friedrich (completed in 1977), commonly known as "Kittel." Hailed by theologians and biblical scholars throughout the world as one of the most significant projects of the century, *TDNT* has become the standard reference work in its field.

"Kittel" came into the Eerdmans fold via a circuitous route in the mid-1960s, shortly after Bill Jr. took over the company. He made his first foray into Edinburgh, determined to meet some of the distinguished Scottish Calvinist biblical scholars living there, none of whom he had notified in advance. He found himself in his hotel room one Sunday night at 9:00, finally getting up the courage needed to make a nervous phone call to the theologian Thomas Torrance.

Torrance insisted that Bill come over then and there. "I spent a couple of hours in his study that night," recalls Bill. "Torrance had signed a deal with Harper and Row, who had acquired rights to publish 'Kittel' in English."

This was to be a massive undertaking, ten volumes with 700-900 pages apiece. The exegesis of even one word could run to sixty columns. The people at Harper and Row wondered whether such a work would prove mind-numbingly impossible to sell. They published a couple of abbreviated volumes to see how they sold, and the results were inconclusive. Harper and Row was tergiversating. It had been Torrance's idea to translate "Kittel" into English, and he believed it would work if done properly. He strongly suggested that Bill go to New York City immediately and tell Harper and Row that Eerdmans would like to publish Kittel. "So that's what I did," Bill recalls. "They laughed at me. Said it wouldn't work. They told me their two volumes hadn't sold well enough to justify the expense."

Harper and Row finally let "Kittel" go. They had purchased an option from Kohlhammer Verlag, the German publisher, which they allowed to lapse. "Now," says Bill, "I had to put up or shut up. So I flew back to Edinburgh, where I met with Geoffrey Bromiley."

I still remember how chilly it was sitting in his church one summer Sunday, shivering in my seersucker suit. At lunch we sat around a fire, it was that cold. Everybody else was wearing overcoats. Bromiley agreed to do the project. He would translate the whole thing for five dollars a page plus a two percent royalty. He'd sit reading the German, and simply type the text in English. He had such a grasp of church history that he'd freely edit out anything he thought the Germans had gotten wrong. Because of Bromiley's generous terms, we were able to sell our earliest editions of "Kittel" for only twenty-five dollars a volume, back when a good car tire sold for the same price.

In 1985, Eerdmans brought out Bromiley's affordable one-volume abridgment of this massive work, affectionately known as

"Little Kittel," though still a mighty single tome in its own right. Jon Pott remembers an occasion when, not wanting to burden his suitcase with it after a book convention, he left a copy of the book in the hotel drawer next to the Gideon Bible "for any erudite guest with a late-night textual worry."

Before "Kittel" was completed, the company began work on a counterpart to that reference set, the *Theological Dictionary of the Old Testament,* a multivolume English edition of *Theologisches Wörterbuch zum Alten Testament,* edited by G. Johannes Botterweck and Helmer Ringgren, which was also to become an Eerdmans "enduring standard." However, in 1975 editors were alerted to serious problems with the translation. After careful scrutiny by contributors and Eerdmans in-house editors, the publisher determined to take bold and unprecedented action. The Eerdmans people asked contributors to review their articles, obtained the original manuscripts by English authors (some had been translated into German and then foolishly retranslated back into English, with terrible results), and started over. Then Eerdmans commissioned Geoffrey W. Bromiley and David E. Green as the new series translators, joined later by Douglas Stott. Those who had purchased the first edition of the first and second volumes were invited to exchange them without cost.

What began, therefore, as critical embarrassment and financial risk ultimately earned the company widespread respect and underscored Eerdmans's reputation for the highest standards of editorial care. And the series, nearing completion under the eye of its longtime editor, Allen Myers, has been a major reference work in the Eerdmans portfolio.

Children's Books

At the end of the 1940s, despite all the intellectual ferment in Christian publishing circles in America (fundamentalism vs. evangelicalism vs. liberalism), along with Eerdmans's productive partnerships with continental and British presses in biblical reference and commentaries, it was still storytelling that best defined the company's offerings. For several years, from about 1946 to 1954, Christian fiction for adults and juveniles and Bible stories for children dominated the catalogs. WBE had long encouraged a steady stream of Christian fiction, though he freely admitted that some of it was not of the highest quality in a literary sense.

In terms of classic children's Bible stories, Catherine Vos's *The Child's Story Bible* was first published in 1934 and remains a perennial bestseller to this day. Then came Marian Schoolland's *Big Book of Bible Stories* and *Marian's Favorite Bible Stories.* There were also the "modern romances" of Paul Hutchens, the creator of the Sugar Creek Gang, and the voluminous and "hilarious wholesome adventures" for young girls from the pen of Bertha B. Moore.

Hutchens's Sugar Creek Gang books were popular Eerdmans titles throughout America in the late forties and fifties, and they made a surprise reappearance on the Eerdmans stage in the eighties. A delegation of Eerdmans representatives, including Bill and his wife, Anita, were attending the annual American Booksellers Association convention banquet, where the dinner speaker was Garrison Keillor. After dinner, Anita had the opportunity to meet Keillor. "Ah, Eerdmans," he said, "the gospel publisher!" It turned out that Keillor's family had owned many Eerdmans books when he was a child, and his personal favorites were the Sugar Creek Gang books.

While the company continued to sell those perennial favorites, especially in the field of children's fiction and Bible stories, the corporate emphasis turned to focus on theology and biblical studies as the years went by, and for several decades children's literature was more an afterthought than a particular emphasis.

A separate catalog for children's books first appeared in 1988. Within a couple of years thereafter, the company set up a department for juveniles under the direction of Amy Eerdmans, Bill's daughter, who had prompted this decision. Since then, this category has matured into a division of the company called Eerdmans Books for Young Readers (EBYR), now headed by Anita Eerdmans, who, in

addition to her marketing duties, oversees the acquisition and publication of about a dozen titles every year, a mix of purchases from
foreign (mostly European) publishers and homegrown projects.
Anita talked about this development:

> When we started Eerdmans Books for Young Readers in the
> 1990s it was because we felt there was a definite lack of high-
> quality religious books for children. What we saw (and in
> some cases what we ourselves had published!) were books
> with inferior art, poor design, and didactic or preachy text.
> Many of them looked like Sunday school papers bound up as
> books. So we set out to produce a small list of books that
> could hold their own with "regular" (i.e., secular) children's
> books. Amy Eerdmans was responsible for launching the im-
> print, and she laid a strong foundation that still serves us well
> today.

For several years — 1988 through the spring of 1995 — new children's books and even backlist titles were "double-listed," that is,
listed in both the children's catalog and the adult announcement
catalog. That practice continued until the fall catalog of 1995, when
plans for EBYR had finally crystallized.

"Once we got our feet wet in children's books," says Anita, "we
discovered how it is an entirely different world of publishing and
selling, with its own customs and rules. It took us a while to figure
out all the things you need to do to get noticed in that world, including getting the attention of the right reviewers, exhibiting at the
right conferences, and submitting books for all the awards and state
lists. Along the way we got to know a lot of wonderful authors and il-
lustrators, which led inevitably to our being offered — and then
publishing — books that were not in any way religious."

The current children's list includes more nonreligious than religious books, and the religion in question is not always Christianity.
A lot of what EBYR publishes, however, even when it is not overtly religious, is eminently suited for use in religious settings or by fami-

lies or teachers who want a story with a deeper, even spiritual meaning. EBYR has found the "secular" world to be a good market for its religion titles, especially basic Bible stories, books of prayers, and stories about saints. Far more EBYR books are sold in the general marketplace than in the specifically religious marketplace.

The year 2008 was a landmark for the EBYR imprint. Of the fourteen new books released, two won important awards from the American Library Association: *A River of Words,* written by Jen Bryant and illustrated by Melissa Sweet, was named a Caldecott Honor Book; *Garmann's Summer,* a translation of a Norwegian book written by Stian Hole, was a Batchelder Honor Book. Winning these awards was very exciting for a relatively small and new imprint, and it brought with it a new level of attention and respect for EBYR. As has been the case throughout the history of the company, the Eerdmans children's imprint continues to mine gold from European publishers: *Our Father* and *Hail Mary,* board books translated from the French; sophisticated picture-book biographies of Klimt, Chagall, and van Gogh from an Italian publisher; and, harking back to the company's Netherlandic roots, picture books *(Willy)* and fiction *(Soldier Bear)* translated from the Dutch language, originally published by Dutch and Belgian publishers.

Of the nonreligious titles that EBYR publishes, the bestselling are stories that have significant meaning, for example, books about refugees *(Four Feet, Two Sandals),* immigrant kids *(My Name Is Sangoel),* civil rights *(The Beatitudes),* and slavery *(Ben and the Emancipation Proclamation).*

The Eerdmans children's publishing program has come a long way from its humble beginnings. But every week, every year, two titles from those beginnings consistently show up among its Top 10 bestsellers: *The Child's Story Bible* (in print since 1934) and *Leading Little Ones to God* (since 1962).

Passing the Torch

Getting a Fix on an Image

Much was in flux at Eerdmans Publishing during the two decades of postwar years — from 1945 to roughly when Bill Eerdmans the younger took over the company in 1963. Of course, much was on hold during the war years (the company did not publish a catalog in 1942 or 1944), not the least of which was the survival of the heir apparent. One thing that was in flux in those years was the image the company was using to portray itself to its customers and potential customers in catalogs and advertising.

The early catalogs, from the 1930s to the war years, had no identifying logo other than the name of the company. These catalogs were basically lists of books, with some pictures of book sets all lined up in a row, and a few pictures of authors. The first postwar logo shows a nicely dressed man reading a book — presumably a pastor, or "preacher," as the Eerdmans promotional copy would have said — seated in a comfortable, high-backed chair next to a bookcase filled with august-looking books. This pleasant, cartoon-like line drawing certainly portrayed the image of the Bible student, preacher, or Christian layman for whom the company believed it had the books. The slogan was: "Books for devotional reading, for

Eerdmans logo used in the late forties

the pastor's study, and for the layman's edification." But the company used that catalog logo only from 1945 through 1950.

The 1946-47 and 1948-49 catalogs still had the comfortable scholar-pastor, but now pictured as a bookend holding up the six-volume set of Jamieson, Fausset, and Brown. The 1948-49 Eerdmans catalog showed a dramatically different look: its cover was a four-color reproduction (the first-ever Eerdmans catalog in color) of the jacket art of Marian Schoolland's *Favorite Bible Stories,* with the Israelite leaders blowing the rams' horns as they enter Canaan. The entire first *half* of that catalog advertised children's books and devo-

Some Eerdmans logos appearing from 1955 to 1964

tional and "inspirational" fiction — that is, before the viewer even gets to any sermon aids or Bible study aids, let alone the meat of theology or apologetics. The new slogan, introduced on that year's catalog cover, was: "Adventures in Good Reading." From 1945 through 1953, the first ten to twelve pages of every catalog, with four or five titles and descriptions per page, displayed Christian fiction and children's books. (From 1951 to 1954 the catalog title was simply "Christian Books," with no logo at all.)

As of 1954, the catalog finally starts off with the more substantive books on the list: the *New Bible Commentary,* the New International Commentary on the New Testament series, F. F. Bruce's *The Spreading Flame,* Merrill Tenney's *The New Testament,* Louis Berkhof's *The Second Coming,* and so on. Pretty much from that year forward, children's books and fiction find themselves transplanted to the back of the cat-

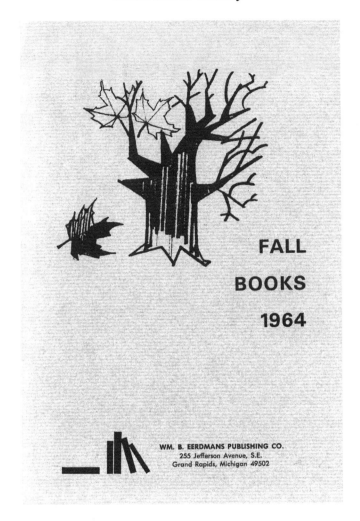

FALL

BOOKS

1964

WM. B. EERDMANS PUBLISHING CO.
255 Jefferson Avenue, S.E.
Grand Rapids, Michigan 49502

The bookshelf-stack logo first appeared in 1964.

alog, even though the company is still self-consciously touting "wholesome Christian books for the entire family."

The 1956 catalog, for the first time, announces new books at the front of the catalog (the first six pages), before it begins the alphabetical listing of the backlist. Adult fiction, biography, and children's books have now found their home in the last ten pages of the catalog. In 1957, for the first time, there are two catalogs: one is an announcement catalog of the new titles, and one contains the entire list, including the backlist. The flux and the searching for a permanent image continued through the 1950s.

Following the postwar catalogs' "reading pastor" logo, there were six different logos and images in effect between 1955 and 1964. The famous bookshelf-stack logo finally emerged in a 1964 catalog, and it has remained the identifying symbol on Eerdmans catalogs and books ever since.

The Van Raalte House

WBE's philanthropic instincts and his interest in the history of the Dutch in West Michigan coalesced in a significant project in 1948. At the urging of the University of Michigan historian Albert Hyma (who had published a history of the world from a Christian perspective and a biography of Calvin with the company), WBE purchased a stately brick house in Holland, Michigan, that had been the home of Albertus Van Raalte (1811-1876), the Calvinist pastor who was the founder and leader of the first Dutch *kolonie* of immigrants in western Michigan in 1847. The house had not been occupied for some time, so he also arranged to have it renovated and restored to good condition, eventually spending the then princely sum of $40,000. He then gave the house to Hope College. His intent was that this house, providing a connection to the earliest experience of Dutch Calvinist immigrants in Michigan, would serve as a repository for important documents and a research and study center.

Within a year, however, the place had been vandalized. Apparently, all the neighborhood youngsters knew about a tunnel that gave access to its interior, and the college did not. Eventually, the administrators of Hope College tore the house down to make room for a sports field. It is a sad story that is told in lacerating detail in a book published by Eerdmans in 2004 (*Albertus and Christina: The Van Raalte Family, Home, and Roots,* by Elton J. Bruins et al.).

Shortly after buying the Van Raalte home, WBE had also acquired an extensive collection of Van Raalte's papers. His purchase of these materials had been facilitated by historian Hyma, who turned out to be a very strange person indeed. In a series of hastily scribbled postcards sent from Ann Arbor or Holland or wherever he happened to be at the moment, Hyma fulminated against the "apostles of Satan," those who would not heed Hyma's advice. At the same time, he was trying to enrich himself by investing in oil wells. Unfortunately, he took investment advice primarily from a medium in Detroit, whose séances apparently provided him with specific information about where to drill. Hyma lost a good deal of money, but he remained something of a genius about gathering papers connected to Van Raalte. On one occasion, for example, he claimed that a voice from the Lord told him to get off the bus and knock on the door of a house near the bus stop. And there he discovered a trove of previously unknown letters from Van Raalte.

WBE set aside a special room for material related to Van Raalte at the company's headquarters on Jefferson Avenue. At one time he had planned to donate this archive to Hope College, assuming it would become a permanent part of that institution's heritage. After all, Van Raalte had donated the land on which the college stood, and he was in every respect its founding spirit. But as the house fell into further disrepair, WBE decided to hold on to the papers. It was 1961 when Hope College finally tore down the Van Raalte home.

William Spoelhof, the president of Calvin College, happened to be driving through Holland on the day of the demolition. He saw a cloud of demolition debris from a distance and knew immediately what it was. So Spoelhof took a detour from his planned itinerary and pulled into the demolition site. He identified himself to the workers, and asked if he could rescue a few items from the rubble. The workers had no problem with that, so Spoelhof took away a desk Van Raalte had used, a few loose papers that were floating in the breeze, some bricks, and two windowpanes, which were later installed in the archives of Calvin College.

At this point, WBE was understandably furious with Hope College. He arranged to give his entire collection of Van Raalte papers and documents to Calvin College, with the proviso that they would remain in Calvin's possession and would never be given to Hope. Around the same time, WBE also made the $10,000 gift that began the Calvin Foundation (now the Meeter Study Center) for the encouragement of Calvinist scholarship.

Editorial Changes

WBE had hired Pete de Visser as editor in the late 1930s: he joined the former in choosing and reading manuscripts, and he ran many of the company's operations, along with Stuart Anderson, the director of sales. De Visser and Bill Jr. did not get along particularly well, so after the war — and after his years at the University of Michigan — the scion of the family spent more than a decade on the road as a "cub salesman," as he always liked to put it, learning the ropes, covering sales territories, getting to know people in seminaries across the country, being introduced to European publishers, and seeking out new books written by religious scholars.

In 1956, de Visser left Eerdmans. For a short time he operated his own publishing company, and he also served as managing editor of the new magazine *Christianity Today,* under Carl Henry. In 1958, Zondervan hired him to be director of publications, and he worked there until his premature death just five years later.

In January 1957, with de Visser's departure, WBE hired Calvin Bulthuis to be the new editorial director. Bulthuis had been an editor at Zondervan for a few years, but according to his close friend George G. (Tom) Harper, he had never felt at home there. "Cal was greatly relieved," says Harper, "when he went to work for Eerdmans." With graduate degrees in English literature and experience teaching at Calvin College, Bulthuis brought a professional literary sensibility to the firm.

Nick Wolterstorff recalls:

Cal Bulthuis was a bit older than I — the age of Lew Smedes and Tom Harper. My primary dealings with Cal were about *The Reformed Journal,* not about Eerdmans business. My impression of him was, to quote Max De Pree, "You have to breathe to live, but you don't live to breathe. The same goes for business and money — you need to make money, but that's not why you're in business." Cal was interested in books, but he didn't ask whether a given book would make money. He asked whether it was a good book. I'm sure someone had to talk about making money, but that was in the background.

Bulthuis was expected to function not only as editor-in-chief at Eerdmans, but also as the editor of *The Reformed Journal,* a monthly magazine that had begun publication in 1951. Henry Zylstra, Henry Stob, Harry Boer, George Stob, and James Daane — Christian Reformed professors, pastors, and friends of long standing — were the first editorial board of the magazine and began the publication with the financial support of WBE. These scholars headed up the progressive wing of Calvin College and Seminary, and they had a feisty belief in lots of animated conversation. The fruits of their conversations, transformed into earnest essays, soon became the heart and soul of *The Reformed Journal.* Their eye was initially on the Christian Reformed Church, but their writing had relevance to people in many other places. The CRC and its problems, it could be said, were paradigmatic of problems within the church worldwide.

"The journal had a distinctive classic-progressive Reformed stance," says Wolterstorff, one of its later contributors and board members. "It was by no means just about American religion. Cal, as editor-in-chief of both Eerdmans and *The Reformed Journal,* put a great deal of energy and time into it. He epitomized the progressive Reformed attitude, and he was gentle and reflective. He loved books, and he had a nose for good writing."

Eventually, the *RJ* acquired a reputation far beyond its initial audience. It was a natural outlet for popular and semipopular essays on a wide range of topics. "No other magazine," said Philip Yancey, "succeeds so well in combining faith and intellect." Carl F. H. Henry, the redoubtable editor of *Christianity Today,* said that *The Reformed Journal* "combines an ecumenical interest with theological and social criticism from a broadly neo-evangelical to neo-orthodox perspective." Stanley Hauerwas called it "the liveliest, most intellectually stimulating, and theologically serious journal being published in America today." Beyond its significance in its own right, the *Journal* had an important symbiotic relationship with the publishing agenda: its editors and authors often contributed significantly to the book program — and vice versa.

But the *RJ* never made money and never had a circulation much over 3,000 (though its fans claimed that it was the most "passed-around" magazine in the religious realm — not uncommon in a largely Dutch reading community). Many readers read it in the library so that they would not have to pay for a subscription. It was also hindered by the fact that its group of founders and its editorial board were made up of academics, who had an impoverished sense of economic realities.

In the early 1990s, Bill Eerdmans decided to end publication of the *Journal.* It had always been something of an orphan within the company. Although it was rich with ideas and controversy, it produced no revenues to speak of (in fact, it drained about $50,000 a year from the corporate coffers), and the job of riding herd on it took valuable time and kept the editor-in-chief of the book program from focusing on other kinds of expansion. Jon Pott, who was the editor at the time of its demise, and also the editor-in-chief of the book program, notes that the end of the company's association with the magazine saddened him greatly, "as I think it probably did Bill."

> I had really wanted it to go on. Nick Wolterstorff and Neal Plantinga and Roy Anker and a host of other contributors thought it was an important part of American intellectual and spiritual life. I called members of the board together and made the announcement, which stunned them at the time;

but most, I think, came to understand. In the end the *RJ* was combined with *Perspectives* magazine, but, inevitably, its character changed. Still, the *Journal* had thrived for forty years, and it had left us with many superb memories.

"To this day," says Nick Wolterstorff, "I have people say to me, 'Too bad about *The Reformed Journal.* And by the way, how can I get a copy of this or that issue?'"

The Quiet Presider

Bulthuis's steady hand, both editorially and personally, was important during the period of transition from father to son, when many competing interests needed to be sorted out. Both father and son trusted him implicitly and admired the professionalism and energy he brought to his work. In one of his letters to WBE, for example — seven dense pages of type — Bulthuis outlined the travels he had made to seminaries around the country during the month of April 1961. He gives a sense of the writers and scholars he has spoken with, painting thumbnail sketches of many of them, and then embarks on a formidable list of forty-one books he believes can emerge from this one cross-country jaunt.

A few examples:

Edward John Carnell (president of Fuller Seminary): "At the moment he is having some difficulty getting on with his book. . . . To say what he feels must be said, he will have to repudiate some of his early upbringing."

Wilbur Smith: "I could not talk him into giving us a manuscript on the English Bible before the one on hermeneutics. He is hot on the hermeneutics. . . . Wilbur is his same enthusiastic self. . . . He is on the verge of becoming the editor of a brand new magazine called *Campus Crusade.*"

**Cal Bulthuis, editor-in-chief, 1957-1971,
painting by Armand Merizon**

Everett Harrison: "Another very fine man and a good worker. He is proceeding nicely with the New Testament part of *ISBE* and at the same time getting on with his introduction to the New Testament."

For some years Cal Bulthuis was the quiet presider over what was often a boisterous bunch of employees. Roger Verhulst, a fine writer, worked in marketing, but he felt himself to be an editor at heart. In fact, he had come to Eerdmans from *Newsweek,* where he had been an editorial assistant; at Eerdmans he coedited, with Glen Peterson, a marketing newsletter called *Inklings,* named after the small group of writing friends surrounding C. S. Lewis. Eerdmans had begun to publish books by and about the Inklings, and the newsletter took on a creative journalistic life of its own. Harold Van't Hof eventually headed up the marketing team, but he, too, had dreams of magnificent possibilities beyond simply marketing. He once tried to persuade Bernadette Devlin, the Irish activist, to write a book for Eerdmans. Marlin Van Elderen, after he got back from a stint in Vietnam, was not boisterous but was endowed with a daunting intelligence. John De Hoog, who had studied at both Calvin and Hartford seminaries, was a language specialist and became the first in-house editor of *ISBE.*

Glen Peterson, who worked in advertising and marketing but was himself a rebel and writer at heart, says that Bulthuis was "a very bright man, very mature, calm, subdued, and often apart from the rest of us, who were still working out our lingering problems of adolescence. Cal was always the voice of reason." He continues:

> I was once at a meeting of booksellers, maybe the Christian Booksellers Association, where Cal was on a panel that was discussing the topic "Good books that still need to be written." I recall the other panel members talking in boring, vague generalities, but Cal went down a list that he had prepared. It was very specific, and each book on his list had specific reasons for why it needed to be written. Each one could take its place in a niche that was then empty. Cal spoke from sketchy notes, but every thought was thoroughly researched and grounded in the basic realities of religious publishing. I remember thinking how I wanted to grow up to be like Cal.

Bulthuis's hiring of a houseful of talented young editors included Jon Pott in 1968, who didn't know how to type and had worried that he had no chance for a job.

> I had interrupted grad school to teach composition and an introduction to literature course in the English department at

Calvin College, and after two years still wasn't eager to return to graduate school. I had seen an ad for an editorial position at Eerdmans in *Chimes* [Calvin's student newspaper], and a few weeks later I applied for the job. This position had opened because Marlin Van Elderen had been drafted into the army — and eventually went to Vietnam. Tom Harper, who was chair of the English department at the time, quickly called his friend Cal Bulthuis to recommend me, and I got the job. I had worried that my inability to type would be a killer, but the issue never came up.

When Marlin returned after two years, I asked Cal whether I could stay, and he said the program had grown enough for it. I had come in 1968, and until 1972 my arrangement with Eerdmans was a yearly thing.

Often there would be an irregular gang of people walking over to the Schnitzelbank restaurant or piled into one or two convertibles and headed to the downtown Peninsular Club or the Great Lakes Shipping Company for a long, sometimes bibulous lunch. Bulthuis didn't drink, even on Fridays, and so he often came across as the most mature member of the group. In the summer of 1969, Eerdmans published Owen Barfield's *The Silver Trumpet*. To celebrate the occasion — not everyone, after all, was able to boast a book by C. S. Lewis's lawyer — Glen Peterson bought a trumpet and took it to a plating company in town to get it coated with silver. But the silver-plating process pretty much dissolved the instrument. It was another experiment that didn't quite work, but the energy was bracing.

The Mantle Descends

Bill regrets that for many years, from about the end of World War II until the early 1960s, he and his father had a difficult time understanding each other.

Excerpt from a feature article in the *Grand Rapids Press,* April 18, 1971 (p. 6), reprinted by permission:

"The Situation at Eerdmans"

Up from the Psychological Hinterland
on a Point of View and a Prayer

by
Steve Hensch

Inside Roger Verhulst's office, the occupant is snapping sarcastic words over the phone to the company's sales manager. Verhulst is Eerdmans' advertising director and, normally, he is a genial fellow. Suddenly, there is an angry squawk from the phone's receiver and then an abrupt click.

"Happens all the time," Verhulst says airily. "We don't believe in memos around here."

Eerdmans is a small firm, which means that memos, when written, aren't lost, and tempers, when stoked, aren't stifled. Eerdmans' top men consider corporations "soulless," and they feel that the small publishing house provides more freedom for its staff members.

"The fun of working here," admits sales manager Harold Van't Hof, "is that everyone has his finger in everyone else's pie."

After that, though, we spent some good times working together. It was a grace that we could walk across the street to the Schnitzelbank, where we'd have lunch and drinks, and we'd talk and come to know each other. After he asked me to head the company [in 1963], I'd always stop by his house and

Which means that Verhulst and Van't Hof can call each other imbeciles over the phone, fume about it for 30 minutes, and then lunch together across the street in the Schnitzelbank Restaurant.

It also means that the company's six full-time salesmen, stationed across the country, can solicit manuscripts; that Verhulst can complain about promotion manager Glen Peterson's latest project; that editor-in-chief Calvin Bulthuis can publish a book that is detested by the rest of the staff.

The result of all this hustling, fighting, and boundary-jumping is books: about religion, about social woes, about Michigan, about famous writers, film directors, and urbanization. The firm also publishes *The Reformed Journal,* an intellectual organ which provides the company with a civilized way to lose money.

The money lost by the *Journal* is covered by the profits made by the rest of the firm. The company's treasurer, Hero Bratt, says: "I can't recall a year since I started working here, in 1938, that this company has lost money." Bratt is one of Eerdmans' two vice-presidents (the other is Bulthuis), and he is a kindly, soft-spoken gentleman who considers himself to be a conservative influence within the firm.

He also feels that he is in the minority, which is probably true, because it is progressive ideas and promises of increased intellectual and national prestige for the house that animate the younger staff members.

tell him what was going on. I remember once, standing with him in the driveway, I opened the trunk of my car and there sat a stack of about a dozen unread manuscripts. I'd gotten behind in my work. He almost collapsed. I beat a hasty retreat and started working at them immediately.

In the first few years after Bill Jr. took over the reins of the company, while Bulthuis provided editorial stability and treasurer Hero Bratt maintained sturdy control of the company's financial health, there were several changes blowing in the wind. The aesthetic design of catalogs and book covers became palpably more modern. As of the 1964 catalog, for example, there was a completely new feel to the catalogs and book covers. Also, the literature on offer was now more characterized by the Inklings than Paul Hutchens and Bertha B. Moore: serious writers like C. S. Lewis *(God in the Dock, The Pilgrim's Regress),* Dorothy Sayers *(The Man Born to Be King, Are Women Human?),* Owen Barfield *(History in English Words),* Stuart Barton Babbage, Kenneth Hamilton, Rod Jellema (editing the Contemporary Writers in Christian Perspective series), and so forth. These trends clearly reflected a changing of the guard.

Bill Jr. and Cal Bulthuis got along very well, and they usually understood, or at least respected, each other's aesthetic sensibilities. However, there were exceptions. Bill remembers one occasion when one of the catalogs had a picture of a Volkswagen on the cover. "Cal was on the verge of resigning," he recalls. "'What in the world does a Volkswagen have to do with serious books?' Cal fumed." Bill thought the ordinariness of the car — its modesty, its participation in everyday life, its funky functionality — could serve as a symbol of the kind of books featured in that catalog. The back of the car also sported a bumper sticker that Eerdmans put out at the time: "I Fight Illiteracy: I Read." Eventually, Cal saw the point of it (or at least stopped protesting), and a later catalog even featured a psychedelic VW van decorated with slogans of the Jesus people.

Both Bill and Cal were behind the change in the nature of the fiction the company was publishing, along with Jon Pott, who was the in-house editor of Rod Jellema's Contemporary Writers in Christian Perspective series. By this time the staff of editors was tremendously important to the shape and content of the work Eerdmans published. By 1971, eight years after Bill took over the company and thirteen years after Cal Bulthuis had taken over the editorial reins, a new spirit had settled in. But an ominous dark cloud was on the near horizon.

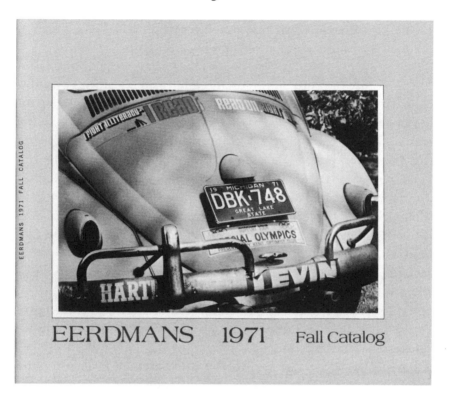

EERDMANS 1971 Fall Catalog

The "Beetle" catalog

Bill Voetberg remembers taking a trip to the South with Bulthuis in the late summer of 1971, not really aware of just how ill the latter was, but noticing that he was very weak. Voetberg thought it may have been overwork, since Cal always drove himself relentlessly. But it was more than overwork. Jon Pott remembers the last few weeks of 1971.

> I remember he went into the hospital around Thanksgiving of 1971. John De Hoog and I visited him there, and we could see that he was concerned about his condition. Exploratory abdominal surgery right after the holiday found cancer everywhere. De Hoog and I had bought some records for him for Christmas, but we couldn't bring ourselves to give them to

him. He died on Christmas Eve. Cal's death was the first big blow in my life. We all loved and respected him.

The sense of youth and vigor and endless possibilities was now changed into a feeling of deep sadness. Cal's passing meant that, for the first time, Bill Jr. would have to make crucial decisions about the company's future more or less on his own. Of course, he sought advice from a few people on his staff, but as he remembers it, Marlin Van Elderen was the obvious choice to succeed Cal. Van Elderen was only twenty-six years old, and had recently returned from a stint in Vietnam, which had followed his first year of graduate work at Harvard University. But Bill had no doubts about his choice. "Despite Marlin's youth, he had the ability and the energy. I was fairly young myself — and full of beans and ideas and visions. This may occasionally have gotten in the way of others, but I shared with Marlin a commitment to ecumenism, to literary excellence, and to a range of social issues that were important to both of us. In this company we retain those commitments to this day."

While Van Elderen was editor, he articulated his goals in a statement that continues to ring true four decades after he made it:

We do not work with a definite statement of purpose, nor do we insist that books appearing under our imprint measure up to this or that standard of orthodoxy. Though the tradition out of which we come is the Reformed or Calvinistic branch of Protestantism, we have published books by and for Catholics, Anabaptists, Pentecostals, Lutherans, Quakers, and Jews. We have published books that call attention to what their authors see as doctrinal errors in other books we have published!

Does that open us to the charge of being wishy-washy, unsure of our commitment? I think not. It has always been our position that we as Christian publishers can best serve the interests of the whole community of believers by drawing our books from a wider spectrum than any of us personally might be comfortable with.

There is a whole range of factors beyond theological stance that goes into our deciding whether or not to publish a book. Usefulness, creativity, integrity, lucidity, importance, sensitivity to significant social and cultural issues — it's not a question of rating the book according to each of these criteria on a scale of 1 to 10 or anything like that. But one does hope for a final product that is in our age of inflated communications genuinely worthy of the time and attention of the people we ask to read it.

From 1972 until 1981, Van Elderen served as vice president and editor-in-chief of Eerdmans. Then Jan Kok, head of publishing for the World Council of Churches, asked him to take a one-year position with the WCC in Geneva. There Van Elderen worked as a temporary replacement for the editor of the WCC's book program. Jon Pott subbed for him as editor-in-chief at Eerdmans and editor of *The Reformed Journal* for the year he was gone. In 1981, Marlin returned from his Geneva assignment to resume his position at Eerdmans. But in 1982 the WCC offered him the prestigious position of editor of its international magazine, *One World*. He decided to take that offer, with the result that Pott took over Marlin's position permanently in late 1982. Of their ongoing relationship Pott says:

> Since we continued to copublish a number of titles with the WCC, it was wonderful for the two of us to have such a close friendship. He was a good fit with the institutional church and thrived on the workings of the World Council of Churches, a center for mainline Christianity. He loved that world and was suited to it. He met a lot of influential people, and he saw a great deal of the world. He was a real workhorse at the World Council and a highly respected analyst and advisor well beyond his area of publication. He probably knew more about the workings and history of the Council than anyone else, but he was under a great deal of stress.

Marlin Van Elderen, editor-in-chief, 1972-1981

On June 12, 2000, Marlin Van Elderen died of a massive heart attack in his home in Geneva at the age of fifty-four, which shocked and saddened his friends and colleagues at Eerdmans and the admiring people whose lives he had touched in the Christian church around the world. At the time of his death he was working on two projects that were to be copublished by Eerdmans. He was the second head editor at Eerdmans to die a premature death.

After beginning as a temporary employee in 1968, Jon Pott has been with Eerdmans for forty-three years. John Updike's death a couple years ago brought back a few of Pott's memories of that faraway era, as he recounts in a recent company blog post observing this anniversary year:

> When John Updike died two years ago this month, I promptly went to the bookstore, lingered over the Updike shelf, and came away with the paperback edition of *Due Considerations,* his final assemblage of nonfiction prose and the sixth such

compilation since *Assorted Prose* in 1965. Most of these volumes are impressively fat. The man was so prodigiously prolific one marveled that he was able to consider much of anything at all duly, a wry irony that might have occurred to him as well when he titled the book.

I bought this latest tome as an act of homage to perhaps the most naturally elegant and felicitous American stylist of our time, that effortless ease — as it seemed — encouraging the output he achieved. I bought the book, too, as a nostalgic tip of the cap to a modest, very occasional, but memorable connection we at Eerdmans had with the man over his long career.

Updike, I'd like to think, had a bit of a soft spot for us. Perhaps he appreciated at least the sheer industry we put into taking his religious seriousness seriously — in no fewer than four critical studies, beginning with a volume in our series in the 1960s and '70s called Contemporary Writers in Christian Perspective, a series of booklets (always six signatures, forty-eight pages) produced in a period for us of literary idealism and, I'm sure, no little romantic pretension. Editing a number of them was one of my happiest early assignments at Eerdmans.

The series included wonderful little introductions to, for example, Flannery O'Connor (by Robert Drake) and C. S. Lewis (by Peter Kreeft), two subjects who brought to the series the helpful benefit of having already died. No one, on the other hand, succeeded in dating a volume in the series more quickly than did Updike, who continued to pour out novel after novel year after year, not to mention the poetry and the essays.

Our CWCP writer on Updike was Kenneth Hamilton, who soon thereafter embarked with his wife, Alice, on a more ambitious critical treatment. Buried somewhere in our archives, waiting to be unearthed in this Eerdmans anniversary year, should be a note from Updike chortling over the coincidence of his working one summer in the Bodleian Library, knowing that only a few carrels to the side, the diligent Hamiltons were laboring away on a second book about him. The book came out under the title *The Elements of John Updike,* and, in a somewhat friskier time for Eerdmans than now, carried a racy (think *Couples*) drawing of Updike by David Levine, courtesy of *The New York Review of Books.*

If Updike's interest in religion made us naturally interested in him, it also made him, however peripherally, aware of us — particularly aware of us as a publisher of Karl Barth. Updike knew and cared more about Barth than did any other important writer — read *A Month of Sundays* — and this occasioned the only writing, besides a blurb or two, that he actually did for us. We were about to publish in English a little volume of pieces by Barth on his great love, Mozart. And knowing of Updike's interest in Barth, but also recalling that he had written a children's adaptation of *The Magic Flute,* we wondered whether he might combine the two interests in a foreword to our Barth book on Mozart. Might we slip our mere sliver of a manuscript under his door for his consideration, we importuned? "Slip it under," came the reply — in full, as I recall, on a postcard with his usual rubber-stamped address.

We may actually have sent him some marked-up proofs instead of a manuscript, because in short order came a foreword and a cover letter beginning, "If you are already in proof stage, then you have no time to waste, and I hasten to send you a few pages prompted by a delighted reading of your little book." Then, later in the letter, came a little Updikian worry: "I hope that my thoughts do not seem overly much to summarize what the reader is about to experience, and that I have not stepped out of line in the tricky theological terrain."

One other Eerdmans story involving a star of the literary firmament concerns the poet W. H. Auden. At the zenith of the successful CWCP series, Bill and the series editor, Rod Jellema (whose collected poems, entitled *Incarnality,* Eerdmans has recently pub-

**Jann Myers with monographs in Eerdmans's
Contemporary Writers in Christian Perspective series;
in the background is the framed cover design for Rod
Jellema's contribution on Peter De Vries; 1971**

lished), found themselves in New York City seeking Auden's walk-up flat on St. Mark's Place in the East Village. Jellema had written a book on Auden, and he wanted to convince Auden to do a booklet on J. R. R. Tolkien for his series. This illustrates another characteristic of Bill Eerdmans: when it comes to seeking prominent authors to write blurbs or even books, his attitude has always been, "Don't say no for them." The two men found the building and rang Auden's apartment on the second floor. A door opened at the top of the stairs, a man in pajamas looked down, and Auden's unmistakable cigarette voice came down: "Just put it there and charge my bill. I'll come down and fetch it later." He had assumed that the publisher and editor were from his dry-cleaning establishment.

When Eerdmans and Jellema had cleared up their identity, Auden asked them up to his flat, and before long he agreed to do the requested booklet on Tolkien. Overjoyed at their good fortune, Bill and Rod Jellema headed to the nearest bar for lunch and a celebratory glass of champagne. Unfortunately, in a subsequent *New Yorker* article, Auden was quoted to the effect that the art he'd seen in Tolkien's home was nothing but kitsch. Tolkien was furious, and Auden withdrew his booklet from the CWCP series. "So," Bill says philosophically, "it didn't happen."

Becoming a Controversial Publisher

A s he talks about the evolution of the company in the years since
1963, when he took over, Bill says, "Although I'm sure I've not
always done it in the best way, I hope I have not only kept my father's
faith, but have expanded it."

In 1946 a young Dutch university student wrote to WBE to thank
him for sending books at a time when the entire nation was struggling to recover from five years of Nazi occupation. The student, the
son of the theologian G. C. Berkouwer, was especially thankful that
WBE had sent a copy of *God's Trombones, Seven Negro Sermons in
Verse,* by James Weldon Johnson (1871-1938), a writer connected
with the Harlem Renaissance, a lawyer, a professor, and an early
leader of the NAACP. "I saw the book in a library once, before the
war," young Berkouwer elaborated, "but I never thought I would
own a copy myself."

Racial Justice

In 1948, as President Truman was ordering the racial integration of
the U.S. armed services, Eerdmans published *Root Out of Dry
Ground,* by Argye M. Briggs, which won the Eerdmans Fiction Award
in 1948 (and the $5,000 cash prize that went with it) — with beauti-
ful illustrations by Reynold Weidenaar, WBE's son-in-law. Briggs

was an Oklahoma writer whose protagonist was a young African-American girl who was struggling with her society but was strong in her faith. This girl believed that Jesus was black, which raised some hackles among the earliest (prepublication) readers of the novel. Several of the editorial readers WBE had sought out raised questions: a Southern adviser wanted to delete any mention of Jesus being black and substitute a statement that Jesus loved children of all colors. (Another adviser, the editor of the Christian Reformed weekly, *The Banner,* was not concerned about race but detected clear signs that the young female protagonist was Arminian, and he suggested ways to correct that heresy in her!)

WBE had great faith in the power of this story, however, and his faith turned out to be well placed. The first printing, of 17,500 copies — an unusually high print run for an unknown author by a publisher not in New York — sold out quickly, and the book was widely read and celebrated throughout America. It became a featured selection of the People's Book Club of Montgomery Ward, a national retailer at the time, which meant it went through multiple printings.

Briggs followed that triumph with *This, My Brother* and *The Hem of His Garment.* On his selling trips through the South, Bill Jr. often visited Argye Briggs and her family in Oklahoma. Her husband was an executive with Philips Oil Company, while she wrote a number of novels for Eerdmans. She was a longtime member of a Southern Baptist church who later in life migrated toward Unitarianism. (As it happens, the late Mrs. Briggs's grandson, Dr. David Hillis, who was named a MacArthur Foundation Fellow in 1999, heads a prestigious department of evolutionary studies at the University of Texas.)

In the late 1960s, racial conflict had exploded on the streets of America, reflecting the desire of black people to be liberated from institutionalized white racism and repression. In 1967, just three years after the changing of the guard at Eerdmans, the company published Charles Fager's *White Reflections on Black Power,* a study of emerging black political manifestations. By 1969, Sterling Tucker, the executive director of the Washington, D.C., Urban League, published a parallel book to Fager's, entitled *Black Reflec-*

tions on White Power. In that same year, Fager, in a book called *Uncertain Resurrection,* wrote about the poor people's Washington campaign. In the spring of 1970, Robert Terry, the associate director of the Detroit Industrial Mission, published *For Whites Only;* and in the fall of that same year, Sterling Tucker answered with *For Blacks Only: Black Strategies for Change in America.*

That period of the late 1960s into the early 1970s brought a whole raft of titles on the subject of race in America, such as *Black Self-Determination* (Arthur Brazier), *Notes on Christian Racism* (Philip Holtrop), *A Culture of Poverty or a Poverty of Culture* (J. Alan Winter), *No Balm in Gilead: Sermons on Racism* (J. Herbert Gilmore), *Black Jargon in White America* (David Claerbaut), and *Blacker Than Thou* (George Napper). One collection of essays, *The Failure and the Hope,* put together by Will Campbell and James Holloway of the Committee of Southern Churchmen, featured an amazing array of contributors, including Walker Percy, John Howard Griffin, Vincent Harding, Thomas Merton, Fannie Lou Hamer, Loyal Jones, and, of course, Campbell and Holloway. Bill Eerdmans also underwrote a journey to Africa by the Grand Rapids African-American artist Paul Collins, which resulted in a coffee-table art book containing Collins's paintings and a text by Tom Lee, entitled *Black Portrait of an African Journey.*

This skein of studies in racial justice culminated in 1982 in the publication of a searing indictment of white racism by Charles H. King Jr., a former Baptist minister and seminary professor who had become a civil rights activist. Bill saw an appearance by King on the Phil Donahue Show and was taken by the latter's strategy of "confronting whites eyeball to eyeball and daring them to suggest anything less of me than they see in each other." Bill telephoned Reinder Van Til, one of his former editors who was at the time a freelance newspaper writer in St. Paul, Minnesota, and asked him to get on a plane to Chicago, where King was conducting one of his corporate seminars on racism in a hotel conference center. Armed with a tape recorder and a notebook, Van Til sought to play the part of a journalist analyzing the Charles King phenomenon from the sidelines. But

King had other ideas: he said that Van Til had no business sitting on the margins, but would have to undergo the same humiliating treatment that all the other white people in the seminar were experiencing (part of King's methodology of exposing white racism). Later in the day, when Van Til said that he needed to check in at the desk, King said, "No, you stay in my room with me." So the white Eerdmans representative and the black civil rights activist got to know each other quite well. King was a master leader of the "group encounter seminar," but he had not bothered to get much of his methodology and his ideas committed to print. But, from a few scattered writings and the recorded proceedings from one of King's three-day encounter sessions, Bill was able to coax out of King and Van Til an analysis of and confrontation with institutional racism entitled *Fire in My Bones.*

South Africa and Apartheid

By the 1970s the world was looking at the problems of South Africa, and the Christian Reformed Church, along with many other American and European Christian groups, was expressing concerns about the policy of *apartheid* there. This was a particularly thorny issue for Calvinists in America. The Dutch-descended Afrikaners who ran South Africa and who had unleashed a brutally repressive set of laws were mostly Calvinists: they had come from the denomination in the Netherlands that was affiliated with the CRC. Rubbing a kind of theological salt in the wound, Afrikaners quoted extensively from the theologian and Dutch prime minister Abraham Kuyper as they were constructing the ideological edifice for their laws and strictures against black people. Kuyper had frequently talked about "sphere sovereignty," developing a method of coexistence within Dutch society that gave independent areas of power to ideologically opposed parties. It was a Netherlandic version of "separate but equal," a policy that the American Supreme Court had repudiated in 1954 in the *Brown v. Board of Education* decision. Nor is it at all clear

Bill Eerdmans, ca. 1978

that Kuyper himself would have approved of such policies. He had often insisted on the equality of all people in the eyes of God. But the battle lines had been drawn, and the most visible Calvinists in South Africa were on the wrong side.

Bill Eerdmans, as a North American publisher with roots in the Dutch Reformed tradition, was determined to address this issue. As early as 1973, Eerdmans published a "Christian cry for racial justice," *Break Down the Walls,* by Johannes Verkuyl, a Dutch missiologist and ecumenist who analyzed in that book the biblical message and the race question, as well as "the gospel of Christ and racial ideology in South Africa" and the "churches' struggle for racial justice." In 1976, the company published *Namibia* by Bishop Colin Winter, a persistent critic of the apartheid regime who became bishop-in-exile when he was removed from his Anglican diocese because of his views. But the program of South African analysis and protest really got cranked up in earnest with the publication in 1979 of John de Gruchy's *The Church Struggle in South Africa,* which went into two editions.

Eerdmans was the first American publisher to give voice to Bishop Desmond Tutu, whose book *Crying in the Wilderness: The Struggle for Justice in South Africa* came out in 1982, followed in 1984 by *Hope and Suffering,* published shortly after he had won the Nobel Peace Prize. The company published other prominent anti-apartheid activists, such as Allan Boesak, Charles Villa-Vicencio, and C. F. Beyers Naudé, as well as a host of theologians and church leaders who were active in the struggle for change in their country. At the height of its South Africa phase — from the spring catalog of 1986 to the fall catalog of 1987 — Eerdmans announced twelve new books that examined apartheid and those fighting it inside and outside South Africa.

Feminism

Linda Bieze, managing editor at Eerdmans since 2003, recalls: "One of the most important books in my life — *All We're Meant to Be,* by Letha Dawson Scanzoni and Nancy A. Hardesty — was picked up by Eerdmans after it had gone out of print. Originally published by Word, in 1974, it was a careful exposition of biblical feminism. I first encountered it while I was in college, and found increasingly more books about feminism from a Christian perspective. Eerdmans's reissue of the book was consistent with its approach to issues such as this."

The mid-seventies also saw Paul Jewett's biblically based landmark study *Man as Male and Female,* and five years later his *The Ordination of Women,* for which he made an argument to a reluctant evangelical audience. In the mid-to-late 1980s, there was a spate of books on Christian feminism, including Elaine Storkey's *What's Right with Feminism* (1986), Anne Atkinson's *Split Image* (1987), and Mary Hayter's *The New Eve in Christ.* These were followed by *After Eden,* written by Mary Stewart Van Leeuwen and a team convened at Calvin College, and later by the massive art book *Great Women of the Bible in Art and Literature,* a lavishly illustrated coffee-table book put together by the German feminist Dorothée Sölle. Also under the rubric of women's voices in the Bible came the large reference volume *Women in Scripture,* edited by Carol Meyers, Toni Craven, and Ross Kraemer, and Marchiene Vroon Rienstra's *Swallow's Nest.*

Religion, Politics, and Cultural Issues

Another area of interest has been the role of religion in politics and the related subject of the relationship between church and state. Prominent among books in this area is *The Naked Public Square* (1984), by Richard John Neuhaus, a book that attracted major media attention in the secular press as well as religious journals. *Political Evangelism,* by Richard Mouw, *Responsible Revolution,* by Canon Michael Hamilton of the Washington National Cathedral, and other publications highlighted a liberal political perspective on matters of the state and the church.

Underlying and supporting this ongoing publishing concern with Christianity and the political order have been many important, foundational books, including those by Oliver O'Donovan (e.g., *The Ways of Judgment* and, with wife Joan Lockwood O'Donovan, *From Irenaeus to Grotius*), Max Stackhouse (e.g., *Creeds, Society, and Human Rights*), and books by Nicholas Wolterstorff, whose *Until Justice and Peace Embrace* became a kind of clarion call for many working in the area of social justice. Eerdmans published Wolterstorff's *Justice in Love* in 2011. One might also note here the important work of Jean Porter on natural law, in particular her *Ministers of the Law* (2010), and the imposing contribution of John Witte and the Emory Center for the Study of Law and Religion.

There were other cultural and social issues that became hot-button issues among the churches — and especially among evangelicals — and the publisher and his editors neither shied away from nor followed an evangelical party line on those issues. As a small sample, on abortion: *Abortion: The Personal Dilemma* (R. F. R. Gardner); on homosexuality: *The Gay Church* (Ronald Enroth and Gerald Jamison) and *Homosexuals in the Christian Fellowship* (David Atkinson), and after the turn of the twenty-first century, *A Time to Embrace* (William Stacy Johnson), a biblical, theological, and legal plea for Christians to embrace gay marriage. In the area of environmentalism, Loren Wilkinson's *Earthkeeping,* along with Wesley Granberg-Michaelson's *Tending the Garden* (1986), were calls for a greener Christian commitment.

Evolution

It was in 1986 that Eerdmans published perhaps its most controversial book up to that time, Howard Van Till's *The Fourth Day.* Van Till was then a physics professor at Calvin College who postulated in his book that the "days" of creation were not necessarily 24-hour periods and that the earth was much older than the 6,000 years claimed by fundamentalists. This view had earlier been articulated by Charles Lyell in his *Principles of Geology,* which had been published in 1830. Yet, a century and a half later, Lyell's ideas were still opposed and denied (indeed, are still opposed) by some conservative, fundamentalist members of the Christian Reformed Church, the church body that runs Calvin College. There were some in that denomination who declared Van Till's views heretical and called for his head.

Leo Peters, a Christian Reformed layman who had made a fortune in the postwar years inventing the red pill and squeezebag that would make white margarine look like butter (he also developed the "Butterball Turkey"), had a history of going after what he took to be liberalism at Calvin College. Peters took out full-page ads in the *Grand Rapids Press* denouncing Van Till and Eerdmans and exposing the heresy. Meanwhile, Tony Diekema, Calvin College's president at the time and a friend of Eerdmans, reported that he spent much of his time after the book's publication "putting out brush fires," as he expressed it, in the Calvin constituency. He needed to appear before one local congregation after another. Peters at one point offered to give a copy of the *The Fourth Day* to every member of every church council in the Christian Reformed Church in order to inform those church officers of the heresy being propagated at Calvin College.

The Eerdmans marketing department saw that offer as the free, heaven-sent advertising opportunity that it was, and they set up a table at the next Synod of the Christian Reformed Church, where they did, as one Eerdmans salesman put it, a "land-office business." *The Fourth Day* was reprinted several times in quick succession while the controversy raged and Van Till was on the hot seat. One of Eerdmans's sales representatives at that time, Carl Ziegler, an éminence grise who had sold books for a number of New York publishers before coming to Eerdmans, expressed an irrefutable publishing maxim during the height of the *Fourth Day* tumult. As a young salesman, Ziegler said, he had sold the new Revised Standard Version of the Bible in the early 1950s. Part of his territory included southern Ohio, where some conservative church groups he sold Bibles to were ceremoniously burning the RSV because of its so-called denial of fundamental biblical doctrines such as the virgin birth (the RSV's translation had changed Mary from a "virgin" to a "young woman"). At an Eerdmans sales meeting where the marketing of Van Till's book was being discussed, Ziegler leaned conspiratorially toward a younger colleague and said in a stage whisper, "They gotta buy 'em to burn 'em."

**Bill Eerdmans and Jon Pott showing strength
and offering mutual encouragement**

Theological Satire

In 1951, two students at Concordia Seminary in St. Louis invented a European thinker whose work they could cite — should the need arise — in their term papers without actually having to look up real sources. Since the student term papers were invariably due on Mondays, and the seminary library was closed on Sundays, they could, without being in the library, footnote their papers with quotes from Franz Bibfeldt, the "distinguished" German theologian who always seemed to have a pertinent paragraph — indeed, a veritable fistful of clichés — at the ready in his vast and virtually impenetrable body of work. One of those students was Martin E. Marty, and it was he who wrote in Concordia's student publication the first published review of an English translation of a Bibfeldt book. "Not since Karl Barth issued his *Romans* from Safenwil has a continental voice sounded so sudden and surprising a theological note," wrote Marty in his review. "A *Pfarrherr* like Barth had been, Bibfeldt has been working until quite recently in relative obscurity in little Grossen-knetten, Oldenburg. To use Sasse's phrase, Barth was 'bone of the liberal theology's bone and flesh of its flesh' when he rose to criticize it. So too the author of *The Relieved Paradox* has come out of the dialectical theology movement to appear as what promises to be its most startling critic." Marty also mentions in the review that Bibfeldt "employs a de-mythologizing in his effort to approximate the *kerygma*."

The prankster seminarians had an inside man at the library who made out card-catalog entries for invented Bibfeldt books, and those cards would always indicate that the books were already checked out — so high was the demand for them — should a professor inquire about them. The only faculty member who knew the source of the chicanery was a young Jaroslav Pelikan, and he did not let on. Even so, Marty and his friend were found out as the creators of the fictional theologian by the Concordia authorities, and Marty was judged to be too "immature and irresponsible" to represent the church in London in an assignment that had awaited him. He was assigned instead to a "salty senior minister" in a south Chicago parish, a man who forcefully recommended that his assistant pastors study toward a doctorate at the Divinity School of The University of Chicago. That punitive Chicago assignment had a dramatic effect on the rest of Marty's career.

Once he had become professor of modern Christian history at the Divinity School, Marty reintroduced Bibfeldt to a wider spectrum of theological professionals — and the German theologian's oeuvre took on a new life. During many academic years, but not all, on the Wednesday nearest April 1st, "the Foundation" sponsored a Bibfeldt memorial luncheon lecture, held at the Divinity School, where irreverent attendees were served beer and bratwursts. Some of those lectures had titles such as "The Quest for the Historical Bibfeldt," "The Politically Correct Fundamentalism of Franz Bibfeldt," "The Breakdown of Consciousness and the Origins of the Quadrilateral Mind," and "There's No Business: Franz Bibfeldt and the Place of Religion in Show Business." Each of the lecturers received $29.95, the annual yield from the Donnelly Stool of Bibfeldt Studies, presented annually by a scion of the famous printing family. These memorial lectures gained such notoriety that presentations and panels on Bibfeldt's theology soon followed at meetings of the American Academy of Religion and other august theological venues.

Martin Marty explains why Bibfeldt is so important as a symbol of twentieth-century theology, why, "for the better half of the last century, international gatherings have awaited his presence and devoted themselves to his words and ways":

> Bibfeldt is "about" Proteanism, as his coat of arms demonstrates [depicting Proteus rampant upon a weathervane, with the inscription: "I dance to the tune that is played"]. He is about being able to affirm and negate, to change. Scholars of Bibfeldt, by studying him carefully, have been able to track one of the main elements in 20th-century theology. One might ask: How could one be a Barthian ("God as Wholly

Other") one year, a death-of-God theologian the next, and a Barthian again a year later? Why is it that so many of the theologians who were on the far left in the late 1960s turned to the right in the 1980s? Bibfeldtians know: it is the *Zeitgeist,* the spirit of the times, to whose whistlings many theologians dance. Bibfeldt is a virtuoso in the theological art of making things come out right, of changing sails to meet the winds, of saving face after it has been slapped by shifts in fashion.

Representatives of the Eerdmans editorial team were lucky enough to be invited by Marty to receive an exclusive viewing of the Bibfeldt *archiv* in the Special Collections section at the University of Chicago's Regenstein Library. In it are the memorial luncheon lectures, publicity photos of celebrity "friends of Bibfeldt" (e.g., Mayor Richard J. Daley and Governor Lester Maddox), proofs of the existence of Bibfeldt, and assorted memorabilia of the great man. This archival treasure convinced Bill Eerdmans to move swiftly and take the bold step of publishing these priceless documents in a *Festschrift* for Bibfeldt entitled *The Unrelieved Paradox: Studies in the Theology of Franz Bibfeldt.* The Eerdmans company followed the publication with a lavish reception for a large gathering of Bibfeldt admirers at the American Academy of Religion and Society of Biblical Literature meetings in Chicago in 1994. Unfortunately, the honoree, who was scheduled to speak at the reception, did not appear for the occasion until a year later. As Marty points out, Bibfeldt has been temporally challenged ever since he wrote his earliest work, his doctoral dissertation, "The Problem of the Year Zero."

Expanding the Vision

I n the mid- to late 1960s, Eerdmans Publishing still had the look and feel of WBE's legacy of Dutch and Dutch-American Reformed theologians, along with evangelical American biblical scholars and interpreters. But with the changes that Bill the Younger brought to the company, the decades of the 1970s and '80s had become dominated by books with a social-political-theological agenda. Eerdmans's acquisitions and editorial policy were always responding to the times; and, true to the Kuyperian tradition from which it sprang, the company was always about transforming culture — via evolution rather than revolution.

In the 1970s and '80s, the political and social issues (civil and human rights, war and peace, liberation theology, social justice, and Christianity and Marxism) were well represented on the Eerdmans list, in books such as Arthur Gish's *The New Left and Christian Radicalism* (1970), John Howard Yoder's *The Politics of Jesus* (1972), James Cone's *Speaking the Truth* (1986), and Cornel West's *Prophetic Fragments* (1987). The playing out of those issues in the late 1980s culminated in the fall of communism on the world stage — and in a spate of books on South Africa from Eerdmans.

In terms of theological scholarship before the 1970s and '80s, the company had departed from Calvinist theology and Reformed epistemology with only a few authors from the ranks of American evangelicalism (e.g., Henry Thiessen's *Lectures in Systematic Theol-*

ogy), evangelical Anglicans in the UK and some Mennonite/Anabaptist and free-church strains in the United States and Canada (e.g., Yoder, William Estep, and Everett Ferguson). The books by Anglicans were often reprints or co-imprints with UK publishers such as Paternoster and Inter-Varsity (that story is told in chapter 11). Now the publisher was moving rather deliberately, and yet self-consciously, away from that narrower path and into ecumenical directions.

Bill recalls saying to Jon Pott at about that time: "If we don't do something, and soon, I'll be leaving the company at the end of my life in pretty much the same condition that my father left it in. I won't have added anything new or original. I want us to be able to focus on the next level, whatever that might mean for our company."

What that meant initially was a cultivation of mainline authors and readers as of the 1990s. It became a question of "how Eerdmans could, without losing its role in the evangelical world, assert itself in the mainline," according to Jon Pott, "which really was always our pedigree, given our origins in the Reformed tradition. But we had to convince mainline people that we *were* traditionalist mainline." This took more work with mainline readers than it did with getting mainline authors to cross over. Some Presbyterians, Lutherans, and Wesleyans were increasingly unhappy with their own denominational presses, whose offerings they felt had become too watered down in theology and too low in their view of Scripture. Pott mentions a conversation with Paul and Elizabeth Achtemeier, stalwart mainline Presbyterians, who said to him, "We're evangelicals, too, you know." Both Achtemeiers published in due course with Eerdmans, Elizabeth with books on biblical preaching and Paul joining Marianne Meye Thompson of Fuller and Joel Green, then of Asbury, on Eerdmans's important textbook *Introducing the New Testament: Its Literature and Theology* (2001).

In the two decades since then, the 1990s and the 2000s, Pott has carefully overseen Eerdmans's emergence from the relative semi-obscurity that some thinkers outside Reformed and evangelical circles had consigned it to. There was never much warrant for such

Jon Pott, editor-in-chief, 1982 to present

stereotyping, but because of its location in Grand Rapids, Eerdmans was often lumped together with the more specifically evangelical publishers in that city. Yet, even though it did not have the narrowness of a denominational publishing house, it had for a time followed a more or less narrow Reformed agenda (which was also an evangelical agenda, at least as perceived by those on the outside looking in). Now the company started to become known not only as a major publisher of more or less progressive Dutch Calvinist and evangelical books, but also of Lutheran books and Catholic materials (from both the conservative and the dissident liberationist wings), of Wesleyans and Pentecostals, of Jews and, recently, Muslims. As such, it became a "bridge" publisher between the evangelical and mainline realms, and between different faiths as well, bridging segments of the religious world that were for decades scarcely able to talk with one another.

To be sure, during the 1970s and '80s, Eerdmans had published a handful of major figures who were not American evangelicals and not from its usual stable of authors, theologians who made an indelible mark on the company's list: the Swiss Reformed theological giant Karl Barth; the quirky French lawyer-theologian Jacques Ellul; the German Lutheran theologian Helmut Thielicke; the Scottish Reformed theologian Thomas F. Torrance; and the British evangelist-theologian Lesslie Newbigin. Thomas Torrance's son, Iain, now president of Princeton Theological Seminary, has maintained a long and fruitful relationship with Eerdmans, continuing the tradition that began when his father first met Bill Eerdmans in Edinburgh. The younger Torrance regularly introduces new potential mainstream authors to the company, as did his predecessor Thomas Gillespie, who was a warm and helpful friend to the company throughout his tenure. George Hunsinger, along with his Princeton colleague Bruce McCormack, has been an important advisor to the company on matters pertaining to Karl Barth, and J. Wentzel Van Huyssteen has been an expert in theology and science. In 2006, Eerdmans published Van Huyssteen's prestigious Gifford Lectures of 2004 under the title *Alone in the World: Human Uniqueness in Science and Theology.* Indeed, Princeton Seminary and, under the leadership of Wallace Alston, Robert Jenson, and William Storrar, the Center of Theological Inquiry have become important resources for the Eerdmans program, along with Emory University and Notre Dame, and divinity schools such as Yale and Duke — these joining Calvin, Fuller, Regent (Vancouver), Wheaton, and the like.

The Christian Life

A number of the most successful Eerdmans books over the years have been oriented to spirituality and the Christian life. D. Martyn Lloyd-Jones's *Spiritual Depression: Its Causes and its Cure,* has, since its publication in 1965, remained a venerable presence on the list, joined recently by a book on anxiety by Allan Cole and a book on the dark night of the soul by Addison Hart. One might also mention here Robert Wennberg's recent book on Christian doubt, called *Faith at the Edge.* Against the dangers of narcissism and of viewing psychology as a substitute religion, Paul Vitz published in 1977 his *Psychology as Religion: The Cult of Self-Worship,* a classic still in print in its second edition.

Nicholas Wolterstorff's *Lament for a Son* (1987), written in the immediate aftermath of the death of his son in a mountain-climbing accident, has been an enduring help to thousands of parents and others dealing with shattering loss. More recently, books by John Philip Newell drawing on the richness of Celtic spirituality have enriched the list, as have the books by Joan Chittister, Megan McKenna, Margaret Silf, and Marva Dawn. Christine Pohl's *Making Room: Re-*

Eerdmans has published about fifteen books by Karl Barth, arguably the preeminent theologian of the twentieth century, between 1976 and 1991, none before his death (T&T Clark, of course, had published the English translation of the unfinished *Church Dogmatics* during Barth's lifetime). Some of the Eerdmans books by Barth are compilations of occasional pieces, sermons, letters to Bultmann, and slight pieces such as his *Wolfgang Amadeus Mozart;* but some of these works are more substantial: *The Christian Life* (a large fragment from the unfinished *Church Dogmatics*), *The Theology of* covering *Hospitality as a Christian Tradition* has done much to help individuals and communities recover that ancient and neglected practice for life today. And Ellen T. Charry, in her *God and the Art of Happiness,* a book both academic and poignantly personal, explores the deep richness of this concept in the Jewish and Christian traditions. A book on recovering the Christian art of dying, by Allen Verhey, will be published in 2011.

As to the lived Christian life, Eerdmans has published a number of sets of personal essays by the likes of Alan Jacobs (most recently, *Wayfaring*), R. R. Reno *(Fighting the Noonday Devil),* and Richard Mouw *(Praying at Burger King).* Philip Yancey's collection *I Was Just Wondering* has delighted readers for over twenty years.

One must note here Eerdmans's long history of publishing memoirs, including, most recently, Lewis Smedes's *My God and I,* Hans Küng's *My Struggle for Freedom,* Rembert Weakland's *Pilgrim in a Pilgrim Church,* Carl Braaten's *Because of Christ,* and Stanley Hauerwas's much-anticipated *Hannah's Child.* In 2011, Eerdmans published Wesley Granberg-Michaelson's story of his own life as an emerging ecumenist, entitled *Unexpected Destinations.*

Schleiermacher, Evangelical Theology, and *The Göttingen Dogmatics* (still incomplete in English). Eerdmans has also published a like number (and still counting) of books *about* Barth, including a *Festschrift* assembled by James McCord and T. H. L. Parker for Barth's eightieth birthday in 1967, the year before he died.

Barth's major students Jürgen Moltmann, Eberhard Jüngel, and Wolfhart Pannenberg have had their direct influence on the Eerdmans list. And two of Moltmann's students, Michael Welker and Miroslav Volf, have contributed in major ways to the Eerdmans list in the first decade of the twenty-first century. One can see, then, a direct continuity through three generations of theologians. It was something of a coup for Eerdmans to get the three-volume systematic theology by Pannenberg in the 2000s. Several denominational presses were interested in publishing that milestone, but Pannenberg specifically chose Eerdmans because, as he expressed it, he wanted to reach an evangelical readership as well as a mainline one.

Beginning in 1970, the Eerdmans list included a dozen books by Jacques Ellul, eight books by Helmut Thielicke (1974 to 1990), seven books by Thomas Torrance (1966 to 1984), and seven books by Lesslie Newbigin (1978 to 2005). Thielicke's *A Little Exercise for Young Theologians* is now in its twenty-fifth printing. These international authors from a variety of Christian traditions had long provided readers a range of thinking well beyond the Calvinist denominational boundaries.

Over the years, Gabriel Fackre has published more than a dozen books with Eerdmans, including those expounding his idea of theology as "story." In addition to his multivolume *The Christian Story,* and other investigations, such as *Christian Basics: A Primer for Pilgrims* (written with Dorothy Fackre) and *Ecumenical Faith in Evangelical Perspective,* Fackre is also the author of *The Promise of Reinhold Niebuhr,* a classic study that was favored by Niebuhr himself. Eerdmans recently published its third edition.

Lutheran

It was quite clear that the elder WBE loved the life and times of Martin Luther and his people: he had published biographies and studies of Luther, usually written by Calvinists! In later years, of course, the Lutheran denominational presses — Concordia for the Missouri Synod Lutherans and Augsburg and Fortress (later combined as Augsburg-Fortress) for the synods that eventually became the ELCA — came in to fill the breach, and they gobbled up anything about

Martin Luther and European and American Lutheranism. Thus were there many years during which Eerdmans did not publish books by, for, or about Lutherans. But, as Eerdmans became more ecumenical and broadened its stable of authors, Lutheran scholars became aware of its list — and began buying Eerdmans books and making inquiries.

By this time Bill had befriended Carl Braaten, Robert Jenson, and Robert Wilken (who later converted to Catholicism). The first two, who called their intra-Lutheran movement Catholic and Evangelical theology, developed a series of books that came out of conversations and colloquia that they coordinated — the proceedings of which Eerdmans published. Braaten and Jenson were such an ongoing theological tag-team in the Eerdmans program that a member of the marketing department whimsically named her two pet office fish after them. Wilken became the general editor of the ongoing series of early church biblical commentaries entitled The Church's Bible. These prominent — but atypical and often protesting — Lutherans were looking for a publishing home hospitable to their theological concerns. Richard John Neuhaus, who had published his very influential book *The Naked Public Square* with Eerdmans in 1984, maintained a strong relationship with Bill and the company, publishing, among other things, his Encounter Series with the company. He, like Wilken, eventually converted to Catholicism.

Having made inroads with at least some Lutheran scholars via those early friends of its program, Eerdmans began pursuing Lutheran authors in seminaries around the Midwest and the country in general. The company displayed its books for Lutheran consumption at as many conferences as they could, and the representatives began to report a great deal of interest from the Lutherans — as though they had never noticed Eerdmans before (which may have been true). Luther Seminary in St. Paul has provided more than twenty-five authors over the past fifteen or twenty years to the Eerdmans program, including Gerhard Forde, Roy Harrisville, Arland Hultgren, Craig Koester, Patrick Keifert, Alan Padgett, and Craig Van Gelder.

Textbooks

Countless Eerdmans volumes have been used over the years as classroom texts, and a number of perennial sellers were created explicitly as such. The LaSor, Hubbard, Bush *Old Testament Survey* and Merrill C. Tenney's *New Testament Survey* have served generations of students and remain in print in revised editions. The same is true of George Eldon Ladd's *Theology of the New Testament* and Henry Thiessen's *Lectures in Systematic Theology.* A number of the books of Anthony Hoekema, among them *The Bible and the Future,* while not created as texts, have often been used as such. Of more recent vintage, N. Clayton Croy's *Primer of Biblical Greek* is widely used, as is the Achtemeier, Green, and Thompson *Introducing the New Testament.* In theology, Daniel Migliore's *Faith Seeking Understanding* remains a favorite seminary text; the same is true on the undergraduate level of Arthur Holmes's *The Idea of a Christian College* and Cornelius Plantinga's *Engaging God's World.* Gilbert Meilaender's *Bioethics* continues as an established text in medical ethics, as does the groundbreaking anthology *On Moral Medicine,*

Roman Catholic

Eerdmans had published a small handful of books for the Catholic market before 1990 — for example, its Mission Trends series (co-published with Paulist Press), the *Documents of Vatican II,* and a couple of books about Catholic pioneers (the Frenchman Lefevre) and martyrs (the Pole Jerzy Popieluszko) — but it was in the 1990s and 2000s that Bill Eerdmans and Jon Pott seriously and self-consciously pursued Catholic theology and ethics. Just before the 1990s began, there was Richard John Neuhaus and those who participated in his an ecumenical venture with Allen Verhey (Reformed) and Stephen Lammers (Catholic) as coeditors. The volume will maintain its ecumenical tradition in the third edition, under the editorial supervision of M. Therese Lysaught (Catholic) and Joseph Kotva (Mennonite). A similar ecumenical collaboration occurs in the parallel textbook anthology *On Moral Business,* masterminded by Max Stackhouse, Dennis McCann, Shirley Roels, and Preston Williams.

Established history textbooks on the Eerdmans list include William R. Estep's *Renaissance and Reformation,* Mark Noll's *A History of Christianity in the United States and Canada,* and Edwin Gaustad's two-volume *Documentary History of Religion in America,* updated by Mark Noll. Eerdmans more recently published a general textbook history of America entitled *Unto a Good Land* (Harrell et al., eds.), and the company's offerings in history include many biographies, among them the volumes in its Library of Religious Biography series. Recent biographies of established critical reputation include Roger Lundin's *Emily Dickinson and the Art of Belief* and Allen Guelzo's *Abraham Lincoln: Redeemer President,* which won the Lincoln Prize for 2000.

periodic colloquia on religion and American culture, which found their way into print in Eerdmans's Encounter series. Neuhaus, a civil-rights and social-justice Lutheran when he first came on board with Eerdmans, later converted to Catholicism and became an acerbic neoconservative who expressed his many beefs with liberalism in his journal *First Things.* But as with his father's friendship with the ever-schismatic and flinty Herman Hoeksema, Bill's friendship with Neuhaus never wavered: he continued to publish Neuhaus until the latter's death in 2009.

Next came David Schindler and his *Ressourcement* program. In this series of books, Schindler wished to make available the pre–Vatican II luminaries — in fact, those who were seen as *anti*–Vatican II churchmen — of the earlier part of the twentieth century: Péguy, von Balthasar, Daniélou, de Lubac, Blondel, and so on. This was right up the alley of the neoconservative Catholic movement of the late twentieth century, some of whose champions had already become Eerdmans authors, including George Weigel and Robert Royal. In fact, the future Pope Benedict XVI, Joseph Ratzinger, was soon (by the mid-1990s) on the Eerdmans list with his little book about creation entitled *In the Beginning.*

That element of Catholicism was probably not too concerned that Eerdmans was also publishing biographies and studies of contemplative monk Thomas Merton and Dorothy Day, founder of the Catholic Worker movement. But they had to have blanched a bit when Eerdmans soon published Vatican bad boy Hans Küng *(My Struggle for Freedom* and his own book on creation, *The Beginning of All Things)* and the controversial nun Joan Chittister *(Heart of Flesh, Scarred by Struggle, Welcome to the Wisdom of the World,* and *The Story of Ruth),* not to mention dissident priests Daniel Berrigan and John Dear, who had made their names in the antiwar protest movement, and the left-leaning, gay Archbishop Rembert Weakland of Milwaukee. One can well imagine Richard Neuhaus shaking his head at the idea that his books occupy the same publisher's bookshelf with these latter, who were always on the activist and progressive edge of Catholicism; but in fact he never offered a word of overt criticism to the company.

This again fit Bill Eerdmans's pattern of developing a publishing company as a forum for ideas — sometimes ideas in direct conflict with each other. Authors seemed to accept this about Eerdmans, even when most other publishers of religious and theological books (including denominational houses and university presses) did not seem to have the same capacity to embrace diversity. The dueling sides of Catholicism have continued on the Eerdmans list for the past two decades, with books by Pope Benedict XVI *(The Fathers of the Church, The Unity of the Church)* and new books about the pope, about the cardinals, and about the history of the church or-

"I'm sorry, sir, but Dostoyevsky is not considered summer
reading. I'll have to ask you to come with me."

ders — found in parallel with continuing publications by Küng,
Chittister, Henri Nouwen, Jean Vanier, and Ron Austin.

Orthodox

Though Eerdmans had published Orthodox authors before the
2000s, such as Vigen Guroian and Anthony Ugolnik, the "Russian
front," as Bill affectionately calls it, did not begin in earnest until
2001. Boris Jakim, the foremost translator of Russian religious
thought into English, encouraged Bill to move in that direction.

With the publication of Paul Valliere's *Modern Russian Theology: Bukharev, Soloviev, Bulgakov: Orthodox Theology in a New Key,* another international foray began. In that same year, Jakim's translation of the early twentieth-century Russian Orthodox theological eminence Sergius Bulgakov's *The Bride of the Lamb* appeared. There followed in quick succession translations of six more Bulgakov texts on the theology of the church, including *The Comforter, Lamb of God, The Burning Bush,* and *Jacob's Ladder,* along with works by Soloviev and Dostoyevsky. This first decade of the twentieth century also saw the release of books on icons of the Orthodox faith by Solrunn Nes (2009), David Bentley Hart's groundbreaking *The Beauty of the Infinite,* and Guroian's *The Melody of Faith* (2010). A recently inked contract for three additional books from David Bentley Hart continues this strand of the company's interest.

Jewish

Eerdmans had released a smattering of books on Judaism during the very late 1980s, including Philip Sigal's *Judaism: Evolution of a Faith,* interfaith dialogue books edited by Jacob Neusner and by Richard John Neuhaus, and the signal publication (and longtime best-seller for Eerdmans), Marvin Wilson's *Our Father Abraham: Jewish Roots of the Christian Faith* (1989). Wilson, because of his nuanced understanding of the Jewish faith, was able to team with Jewish writers and scholars on other collaborations involving interfaith dialogue, and Eerdmans became one of the leading publishers of that discussion. Aside from explicit efforts to encourage Christian-Jewish dialogue, Eerdmans published many Jewish scholars and rabbis, including Rabbi Philip Sigal, Rabbi Leon Klenicki, Dan Cohn-Sherbok, Michael Fox, Baruch Halpern, Rabbi Byron Sherwin, David Novak, and Lawrence Schiffman.

The company's approach to ecumenism has always aimed for a three-dimensional view of differing faiths, not simply a series of conversations among various believers. To that end, it has worked

"No, I haven't read the New Testament, but I did read the
Old Testament, and I liked it very, very much."

to acquire additional works about modern Jewish ethics and spiritual practice (Byron Sherwin), biblical psychology (Kalman Kaplan and Matthew Schwartz), and narratives of Holocaust survivors: Theo Tschuy's *Dangerous Diplomacy: The Story of Carl Lutz; The Letters of Etty Hillesum;* Inge Bleier's *Inge: A Girl's Journey through Nazi Europe;* and Eva Schloss's *Eva's Story.* Related to the Holocaust books written by Jewish authors is Diet Eman's *Things We Couldn't Say,* the story of her participation in the Dutch resistance that tried, often at terrible personal risk, to protect Jews. Her fiancé and all eight members of their underground group lost their lives, and for her own heroism she is named among the "Righteous Gentiles" recognized at the Yad Vashem Museum in Jerusalem.

While publishing a good number of these discussions of modern Jewish-Christian dialogue, Eerdmans's growing number of leading scholars in the discipline of Hebrew Bible — its literature, culture, and historical backgrounds — were, under the leadership of Allen Myers, developing a library of the most significant books in the general areas of early Judaism and Ancient Near East studies: James VanderKam's *An Introduction to Early Judaism* (2000); John Collins's *The Apocalyptic Imagination;* Michael Stone's *Ancient Judaism;* Baruch Halpern's *David's Secret Demons;* William Dever's *Who Were the Early Israelites, and Where Did they Come From?* and *Did God Have a Wife? Archaeology and Folk Religion in Ancient Israel;* David Flusser's *Judaism of the Second Temple Period;* Johanna van Wijk-Bos's *Making Wise the Simple: The Torah in Christian Faith and Practice;* David Instone-Brewer's *Traditions of the Rabbis from the Era of the New Testament;* and Gabriel Boccaccini's *Roots of Rabbinic Judaism: An Intellectual History from Ezekiel to Daniel.* Recently, the company published its imposing *Dictionary of Early Judaism,* coedited by John Collins of Yale and Daniel Harlow, a former Eerdmans editor now teaching at Calvin College.

As Christian and Jewish biblical scholars became more collegial and began to work together more collaboratively, Eerdmans became serious about publishing the results of their joint efforts.

Dead Sea Scrolls

Along with those studies in early Judaism, Eerdmans became, during the decade of the 2000s, a leading publisher of material on the Dead Sea Scrolls (DSS), again, much of this under the supervisory eye of Allen Myers. This included both a translation of the Scrolls themselves by Spanish scholar Florentino García Martínez and his massive study edition. The premier DSS guidebook for general readers is James VanderKam's *The Dead Sea Scrolls Today* (1994; 2nd ed., 2010), which won the Biblical Archaeology Society's "best popular book" award in 1995. Other significant studies in this area are Eugene Ulrich's *The Dead Sea Scrolls and the Origins of the Bible* (1999);

Jodi Magness's *The Archaeology of Qumran and the Dead Sea Scrolls* (2002); Peter Flint's *The Bible and Qumran* (2001); and *What Are the Dead Sea Scrolls, and Why Do They Matter?* (2007), by David Noel Freedman and Pam Fox Kuhlken. At any given time, there are fifteen to twenty books on the Dead Sea Scrolls on the Eerdmans backlist. And there are always another twenty books or so under the subject listing "Second Temple Judaism."

Early Christianity

The concern with early Judaism has related closely, of course, to studies in early Christianity and the New Testament and has yielded much important work in the Eerdmans program by significant scholars such as Kurt and Barbara Aland, James D. G. Dunn, Richard Bauckham, Larry Hurtado, Everett Ferguson, Pheme Perkins, N. T. Wright, Richard Burridge, and James Charlesworth, to name only a few.

Islam

The 2000s, whose beginning brought the issue of worldwide Islam into sharper focus, also brought the issue to the editorial desks at Eerdmans. All the way back in 1981, the company had published Kateregga and Shenk's *Islam and Christianity: A Dialogue,* as well as Herman Bavinck's *The Church Between Temple and Mosque.* Thirty years later, in the late 2000s and early 2010s, it had become important for American Christians and Jews to understand the faith of these other "people of the book."

Eerdmans's long history of ecumenical interests has recently resulted in a number of books relating to the Islamic faith and traditions. Norman Hjelm, the former director of Fortress Press, the Lutheran Church's publishing arm, has been a longtime friend of Bill Eerdmans and others in the company. Over the years he has also

**A serious exchange of ideas with the Dutch publisher Kok
in a restaurant in Kampen. Seated to the right is Wim
Steunenberg, Kok's longtime publishing director.**

helped the company acquire books by important Scandinavian
theologians. As Bill puts it, "In any of our recent catalogs, there are
at least four or five titles he got for us." William Rusch, a professor of
church history and ecumenism at Yale, has often worked in con-
junction with Hjelm, and several of Eerdmans' recent publications
on Islam have come by way of recommendations from Hjelm or
Rusch: *Introduction to the Islamic Faith,* by Brian Lawrence; *Islam: A
Short Guide to the Faith,* edited by Roger Allen and Shawkat M.
Toorawa; and *Woman, Man, and God in Modern Islam,* by Theodore
Friend. These join *Islam: Friend or Foe?* by Emilio Platti; *Muhammad,
Prophet of God,* by Daniel Peterson; and *A Common Word: Muslims
and Christians on Loving God and Neighbor,* edited by Miroslav Volf,

Prince Ghazi bin Muhammad bin Talal, and Melissa Yarrington. Bill Eerdmans expresses it this way: "We need a road on which Christians and Muslims under God can travel together as peacemakers on a warring planet."

Ecumenism

Eerdmans's long interest in ecumenism involved a close relationship with the World Council of Churches (WCC), which was encouraged by its Dutch connection with Jan Kok, longtime friend of the company and scion of the Kok Publishing House of Kampen, the Netherlands. Kok had left his family's publishing concern to work in the publications division of the World Council of Churches in Geneva. This collaboration with the WCC continued more vigorously after Marlin Van Elderen left Eerdmans to join the Council. Eerdmans published two books by Geoffrey Wainwright of Duke Divinity School (*The Ecumenical Moment* [1983] and, as editor, *The Dictionary of the Ecumenical Movement* [1991; rev. 1998]) and two by Michael Kinnamon (*Truth in Community* [1988] and *The Ecumenical Movement* [1996]). Also on the ecumenism list was Robert Bilheimer's *Breakthrough: The Emergence of the Ecumenical Tradition* (1989) and Alan P. Sell's *Allies for the Truth* (1990). Eerdmans published all these books — and more — in collaboration with and under the co-imprint of Eerdmans and the WCC. Van Elderen himself contributed two books that were jointly published by Eerdmans and the WCC: *Introducing the World Council of Churches* (1991) and *Finding a Voice* (2001, posthumously).

Eerdmans's interest in ecumenism has coincided naturally with an interest in missions and global Christianity, dating back to the work of J. H. Bavinck and Johannes Verkuyl and including two parallel older series in mission, reflecting respectively mainline and evangelical perspectives. One of them was edited by R. Pierce Beaver of the University of Chicago Divinity School and the other by Donald McGavran of Fuller Theological Seminary. Among other books

The Preacher and Pastor

Books aimed at the preacher and pastor have always played a central role in the Eerdmans program, from commentaries (including the venerable *Pulpit Commentary, Expositor's Bible,* and the works of Keil and Delitzsch) to other reference works; from books on pastoral practice to books on preaching — including the model collections of sermons themselves by some of the world's most distinguished pulpiteers. The sermons of David H. C. Read of Madison Avenue Presbyterian Church in New York and those of Austin Farrer, a splendid philosopher of religion at Oxford, came out in the 60s and 70s, as did the magnificent sermons by C. S. Lewis collected in *The Weight of Glory.* Such have been joined in recent years by the sermons of noted preachers like Presbyterian James Kay, the Episcopal priest Fleming Rutledge, her Anglican counterpart, Oliver O'Donovan, and the Baptist scholar of literature and faith Ralph Woods. In 2003, the company published a treasury of the sermons of Phillips Brooks, the famed minister of Trinity Church in Boston, selected by Ellen Wilbur and introduced by Peter Gomes. One might also note here *This Incomplete One,* a moving volume of sermons occasioned by the death of a young person, selected by Michael D. Bush.

Collections of model sermons, including a fine textbook anthology edited by Thomas Long and Cornelius Plantinga Jr., *A Chorus of Witnesses,* have been augmented by explicit aids to preaching, such as the recent Eerdmans three-volume Lectionary Commentary edited by Roger Van Harn, and, among others, the volumes by Sidney Greidanus on preaching Christ from the Old Testament. A classic on the

Eerdmans list is John Stott's *Between Two Worlds: The Challenge of Preaching Today,* as pertinent now as it was when first issued in 1982 under the title *I Believe in Preaching.*

In the history of preaching, one might note from the current time such books as Richard Lischer's *The Company of Preachers* and Hughes Oliphant Old's magisterial *The Reading and Preaching of the Scriptures in the Worship of the Christian Church,* a seven-volume, one-man tour-de-force by a major contemporary scholar of homiletics and worship.

Aids to pastoral work have notably included the three venerable manuals by Perry Biddle on marriage, hospital visitation, and funerals; the Jesse McNeil *Minister's Service Book;* the books by Lawrence Farris, Deborah Van Deusen Hunsinger *(Pray Without Ceasing: Revitalizing Pastoral Care),* Christian Scharen *(Faith as a Way of Life: A Vision for Pastoral Leadership),* and Michael Jinkins *(Letters to New Pastors);* and the various volumes in the Pulpit and Pew series supervised at the Duke University Divinity School. The vignettes of pastoral life written by Lillian Daniel and Martin Copenhaver and published in 2010 under the title *This Odd and Wondrous Calling* have proved an immediate success with pastors seeking wisdom and replenishment in their daily, sometimes draining, work.

Special note must be made of the work of Eugene Peterson, whose numerous books with Eerdmans, beginning with *Working the Angles: The Shape of Pastoral Integrity* (1989), have been a boon to so many preachers and pastors needing and wanting to be reminded of their central calling. Peterson's five-volume series on spiritual theology is a landmark in the Eerdmans program and is destined to be a gift to pastors and thoughtful laity alike for years to come.

along the way, Eerdmans published in 1998 a comprehensive *Bio-graphical Dictionary of Christian Missions,* edited by Gerald H. Anderson of the Overseas Ministries Study Center. Ongoing in the program today is the Studies in the History of Christian Missions series, coedited by Robert Frykenberg and Brian Stanley. In connection with mission one must also note the seminal contributions of Lesslie Newbigin (especially, perhaps, *The Gospel in a Pluralist Society,* first published jointly with the WCC) and the subsequent work of George Hunsberger, Darrell Guder, and Craig Van Gelder in The Gospel and Our Culture and The Missional Church series. And in connection with Christianity worldwide, one might note the recent five-volume Eerdmans *Encyclopedia of Christianity,* a translation and significant revision of the German *Evangelisches Kirchenlexikon* (Vandenhoeck & Ruprecht), for which Edgar Smith and Craig Noll were the staff editors.

Again, this interest in and anointing of the ecumenical agenda could be seen as a bold and somewhat peculiar move for a company whose bread had been buttered by evangelicalism for so many years, especially since evangelicals at that time usually considered the National Council of Churches in the United States anathema, let alone the WCC, the world body. Dispensationalists and other fundamentalists often viewed the WCC as in the same league with the United Nations — a horrifying conspiracy to impose one-world government (as hair-raisingly portrayed in the *Left Behind* books and movies). Yet this ecumenical impulse by the publisher, as Jon Pott and Bill Eerdmans point out, has been at the heart of the company's mission since the days of William B. Eerdmans père.

The Cutting Edge of Evangelicalism

Even as it was publishing books by ecumenists, liberation theologians, dissident nuns and priests, and those advocating gay marriage, the latter-day Eerdmans editorial group — like the founder, WBE — did not turn its back on evangelicalism. In the mid-1990s, in

**Bill Eerdmans with an armful of Evangelical
Christian Publishers Association awards**

fact, the company published a series of books by authors who were
luminaries in that sector, an appropriate — if edgy — fit in the evangelical world, writers who were central to evangelical intellectual re-
newal during that period. Two of the best known were David Wells's
God in the Wasteland and Mark Noll's *The Scandal of the Evangelical
Mind,* both published in the fall of 1994 and both elaborations and
further probings of compelling themes in Wells's widely read *No
Place for Truth* (1993). Cornelius Plantinga Jr. followed within a year
with a phenomenon that perhaps can only happen in the evangeli-

cal world, a best-selling book on sin, *Not the Way It's Supposed to Be: A Breviary of Sin* (1995).

This series of evangelical calls to arms and a new kind of reformation was stimulated by an initiative to renew evangelical theology, supported by the Pew Foundation. The books eventually published through Eerdmans came to include two more titles by David Wells; and recent books in the same vein are D. A. Carson's *Christ and Culture Revisited*, to be followed by *The Intolerance of Tolerance* in 2012, along with Noll's sequel to his landmark *Scandal*, entitled *Jesus Christ and the Life of the Mind*, published in 2011. These scholars and church leaders, among many, have unapologetically espoused an evangelical agenda and have become clarion voices in the evangelical intellectual world as best-selling Eerdmans authors in the 1990s and 2000s.

Onward and Outward

Out with the Old

It was a strange thing in a way for Eerdmans to have its own manufacturing plant, which did both printing and bookbinding. In the late 1940s Eerdmans bought an independent printing business that happened to be located next door to the Jefferson Avenue offices. "That business had gone aground," says Bill, "but my father depended on it so much that he took it over." The company had not included a bindery, something WBE thought important to his enterprise. He hired Jack Haga from Holland, Michigan, to set one up. Haga installed the necessary machinery and trained the workers, so eventually Eerdmans could do the entire operation under one roof. For a few years the printing part of the business was a joint operation with Cushing Malloy of Ann Arbor. However, after a big fire in the plant, and the installation of new equipment, Eerdmans bought out the Ann Arbor company and took over the entire operation. "That fire was the temporary salvation of the printing operation," recalls Bill. "We'd been saddled with an older technology that required far too much work." The fire destroyed machines that were on their way out anyway, and allowed another several decades of life for Eerdmans Printing Company.

As the printing trade became more sophisticated and competitive over the decades, however, it became more difficult for this related business to survive. Under the leadership, for many of its years, of Frank Bednarsky and Art Anthony, it printed books for Zondervan and other local publishers — Kregel, for example — and also for publishers in Illinois and Indiana, and sometimes even for large New York publishers. But it became increasingly difficult to keep Eerdmans Printing Company competitive. It was necessary to attract outside work to keep the enterprise viable, but there was a constant temptation to put in-house work on the back burner (since the outside companies paid hard cash), and thus to allow some of Eerdmans's own publishing projects to languish a bit longer than they should have.

For years, Bill resisted the idea that the printing plant should be closed. He felt a strong commitment to the men and women who worked there. But he was finally persuaded of the necessity of closing that business down. It had never been the core of the enterprise, which was always publishing, not manufacturing. And so the Eerdmans Printing Company was finally liquidated in 2004.

Claire VanderKam, vice president and treasurer, says it was crucial "to make sure that the employees were treated well — many of them had been with us for decades. We developed a generous severance package for them, and Bill felt that, since this is a family enterprise, it was his responsibility to give the word personally." He felt terrible about having to put fifty-two people out of work. When it came time to announce the closing, Bill walked the few strides down Jefferson Avenue to the plant (accompanied by VanderKam and a consultant they had hired), and made the announcement himself. He took great pains to give the compelling reasons for the closure. He was surprised and touched by the grace with which the employees greeted the news.

Production Technology

Klaas Wolterstorff, the production manager, has seen many changes in the nature of book production during his years with the company.

When I started in 1984, we managed the typesetting, but we didn't do it in-house. We would send out manuscripts that editors had marked up to be rekeyed. Around that time we brought our first computers in and decided to capture all those keystrokes instead of redoing them. We sent out the files to the typesetters on floppy disks — this was still in the early days of desktop computers. They would sometimes send back galley sheets, not even made up into pages, that would have to be cut and pasted up manually, with layers of waxed photographic paper. Each change, large or small, would be pasted down in another layer. I didn't exactly enjoy that, but things did change.

In 1986 we bought a laser printer. It was extremely slow, but we started thinking about doing our own typesetting in-house — at least for a few books. Because those early laser printers were such low resolution, we did everything at a very large size, and the printer would then shoot a reduced version to make film to print from. That saved us enough money that we decided to do the same thing for most of our books. As it happens, we started out with PCs in the editorial department, so we chose a PC-based application for typesetting. In the process, we became one of the few publishing houses not using Macintoshes for what was then called desktop publishing. With Tim Straayer leading the way, we also created most of our own fonts for Greek and Hebrew, and the fonts used for transliteration.

The Move

As for the sale of the property to St. Mary's Hospital, that, too, entailed some painful moments. The company had held forth at its Jefferson Avenue address for almost sixty years. The Schnitzelbank restaurant, a few doors to the south and on the other side of Jefferson Avenue, held six decades of fond memories of friendships forged

Corporate offices on Jefferson Avenue

and solidified, of meals and ideas and an unrecreatable atmosphere of *Gemütlichkeit*. For years Eerdmans employees had affectionately referred to Der Schnitz as the "south office." All that was coming to an end. Karl Gustav Siebert, the Schnitzelbank's proprietor, was ill, and he had also decided to sell his property (which now belongs to the Mary Free Bed Rehabilitation Center). "We stayed in touch with him throughout the last years of his life," says Bill, "sometimes meeting up with him at Rose's Restaurant." At Rose's, "Bill Koski's five-star kitchen and spirited waitstaff serve up grilled shrimp sliders, while heard-it-all-and-grin-and-bear-it bartenders concoct up-and-dirty martinis with eyebrows [anchovies]." Almost immediately, Rose's became the new Schnitzelbank, a favorite place for company lunches.

"When St. Mary's Hospital came after our property," Bill recalls, "I was not going to sell it cheap. I told the hospital's agent that I knew he couldn't expand in any direction other than ours, and I told

Bill in his Jefferson Avenue office shortly before the big move

him that he was, in effect, looking at ocean-front property when he stared longingly across the street at our buildings." Indeed, the company was sitting on a fairly significant expanse of "ocean-front property." The hospital had been after it for a while, but Bill and Claire VanderKam considered their early offers insufficient.

"Their agents came back again," says VanderKam, "talked to me about it, and finally I presented an offer from them to Bill and Anita Eerdmans. We talked some more. Eventually, St. Mary's bought the entire property — about two city blocks — phasing it in while we searched for a suitable place to move to."

That sale and the subsequent move were hard for Bill. He had known that location as the company's home since he returned from World War II, and had had his office there for about forty-five years. His longtime assistant, Millie Gritter, who had come to Eerdmans from Zondervan decades earlier, retired just before the closing of the Jefferson Avenue office. At Zondervan she had served as secretary to Bill's cousin Bernie. When she moved to the competition in the late 1960s, she became Bill's principal assistant, running his office for more than thirty years. She understood the pattern behind the mountains of paper that looked to be pure chaos; she understood the importance of a principle of organization; and she understood Bill's working strategies and his occasional quirks.

In with the New

The sale of the Eerdmans property on Jefferson was completed in 2006, before the collapse of the real estate market. The new building on Oak Industrial Drive created, for the first time in Eerdmans's history, an environment specifically intended for publishing. After years of occupying the altered premises of an automobile dealership, the Eerdmans employees were finally going to get a home that was specifically designed for their purposes. There would be no more mysterious rumblings as a forklift loaded with books made its way overhead.

"When I started working here," recalls Linda Bieze, "the Jefferson building was tumbling down around us, and we sort of laughed about it. We hoped the fire marshal wouldn't check on us. Four editors, for example, worked in the basement. They were all men, so I called them the 'basement boys.' The warehouse was on the second story, above the offices. That floor had been strong enough to hold cars, so it also worked for holding books. I was convinced that the heaviest commentaries were right above my head, because now and then there'd be a deep thud and dust would settle down around me."

Back in the late 1970s the company had done a major renovation of the Jefferson Avenue building, and they did it while people kept working. The construction crews were beating on beams and concrete while editors and proofreaders tried to concentrate. The noise and the dust were sometimes overwhelming. Claire Vander-Kam recalls:

Corporate offices on Oak Industrial Drive

There we were trying to make do — all the time. Here on Oak Industrial Drive, on the other hand, we acquired an empty shell: four walls and a dirt floor. We added a second story, which required additional foundations, and from there we had a blank slate. We could design what we wanted. We had entertained the idea of buying land and putting up a building from scratch. But this was sort of a godsend; and it's in a Renaissance zone, so we got a nice tax break besides.

The acquisition of the new building gave the company an opportunity for once to stand back, take a good look, and get an architectural firm to help it lay out the building efficiently. Representatives from Integrated Architecture went around the old premises and asked questions, looked at what needed to be done, gathered some more information, and then suggested how they thought the new building should be laid out.

"We made a few minor changes in what they recommended," says VanderKam. "For the most part we accepted what they offered. Since the architects were independent of our operations, their suggestions were completely impartial and based solely on workflow and use of space. We went from makeshift offices in a dark, old building furnished with a wide variety of mismatched furniture that had been accumulated over the years to an open and efficient workplace with lots of natural light and matching furniture! It's been great."

Throughout the construction process, VanderKam kept a close eye on the proceedings, functioning as an ad hoc deputy foreman for the construction crew. He saw to it that the work was done according to a carefully planned schedule. The project came in on time and under budget.

In the Warehouse

The operation on Jefferson Avenue had always required a certain amount of logistical improvisation. The warehouse, for example, included three outbuildings, none of which had a racking system. All the books were double-stacked, and shipping access was frequently difficult, calling for more creativity than expected. For forty-two years, until 1998, Rich Watson had worked in the warehouse; for decades he'd been the shipping manager. He had met his wife, Donna, in 1956, when she worked in the mailroom; they married two years later. Five of the six Watson children eventually worked for the company full- or part-time. In 1998, at the age of 71, Rich Watson suffered a heart attack while vacationing in Florida, so he decided it was time to retire. In very short order, his son Duane Watson was appointed the new shipping and receiving manager. It was a smooth transition. Rich died in 2010, twelve years after retiring.

When the company began working on its new building, the architects came to Duane to ask how much room he would need. He drew up some plans and gave them estimates, which resulted in a new warehouse with none of the old drawbacks and all sorts of new efficiencies. There was also room for growth, the luxury of empty spaces. That soon changed, and the warehouse is now fully occupied, but it is much more efficient than the old place was. Duane is not at all nostalgic about the Jefferson Avenue shipping room. The younger Watson loves his work: he's now been at it for twenty-two years, not counting three years as a part-timer while he was in high school. And a third generation of his family — his nephew Dustin Rawson — was part of the Eerdmans workforce from 2007 to 2011.

Financial Stability

Throughout the company's existence it was of great importance that Hero Bratt, the first treasurer — and after him, Claire VanderKam — maintained a steady vision of economic realities for the company. Their stability and practicality made it possible for the editors and the publisher to pursue projects that did not always make economic sense. The two treasurers maintained a long-term vision about the viability of the company, making clear when austerity was necessary, and supporting a corporate culture that does not publish books simply to make money, but that makes money in order to publish books — sometimes provocative or creative or surprising or unpredictable books — while remaining solvent. VanderKam, who succeeded Bratt, describes his former boss:

> Hero was a classic conservative financial officer. He watched the company's money closely, making sure it was used as efficiently as possible. He always said, "Handle the company's money as you would your own." He instilled a lot of that in me. Today, Hero would be called tight, but that would be by those who have no appreciation for his life experience. Hero was from the old school: a Dutch Calvinist with a Depression-era mentality. Growing up, he was forced to make do with less, and less was okay.

Bill Voetberg, who was sales manager during the early 1970s, remembers an occasion when his secretary needed a new typewriter. "Hero found her a used manual typewriter without a functioning letter *o*. I told him that was completely unworkable, that she needed an

175

IBM Selectric, which was the top of the line at the time. Hero looked around some more, and finally found a reconditioned Selectric for $80."

It was Hero Bratt who hired Claire VanderKam straight out of high school in 1970. VanderKam started out opening the mail, the job he had applied for. Within a very short time, however, he moved up to running the computer, using punch cards and mastering the soon-to-be-obsolete technology of the era. Then his duties expanded to include order entry and customer service. In his free time, he offered to help out Al Figg, who was the assistant treasurer. In those days all the ledgers were kept by hand, and all data entry was by hand. Claire worked under Figg for a while, doing more and more bookkeeping. Then one summer Figg had some health issues.

"I was serving in the National Guard at the time," Claire recalls, "and Bill Eerdmans called me, said Al was ill, and asked me to come back right away. Nothing happens quickly in the military, and it soon became clear that the National Guard wouldn't allow an immediate return, so that took a while."

When Claire returned, he was promoted to Al's job of assistant treasurer. Then, in the mid-1970s, Hero Bratt retired. Meanwhile, Claire became, at the age of twenty-three, an officer of the company; before long, in 1975, he was appointed vice president/treasurer.

"Over the years," says Claire, "I had learned a great deal about the business, doing all the small tasks that made sure money flowed properly. It was good training." In the autumn of 2010 he celebrated his fortieth year with the company.

One of Claire's important responsibilities in the past sixteen years has been his role as Eerdmans corporate representative with Alban Books, the distributor it co-owns with several other American publishers. After several years of various fragmented arrangements to sell into the UK/European market, Eerdmans concluded that none of the UK or European publishers provided an adequate solution to represent and distribute Eerdmans's growing list of books. It was also clear from discussions with colleagues from other U.S. publishers that they had similar experiences and were also looking for a better solution. Therefore, in 1995, Eerdmans, along with the publishers Abingdon, Augsburg-Fortress, Crossroad, and Orbis, formed a UK subsidiary, Alban Books, Ltd. Alban, located in Edinburgh, is a full-service sales and distribution organization that answers the need for integrated service using local expertise across the full spectrum of sales, marketing, stock management, distribution, pricing, and customer service. Jane Grounsell joined Alban as managing director in 2000 and continued in that capacity until her untimely death in September 2010, after a two-year struggle with brain cancer. Jonny Gallant was recently appointed as managing director for Alban Books.

In addition to providing their services over the past sixteen years to the owner-publishers (Crossroad Publishing withdrew in 2007), Alban has had distribution arrangements with various client publishers, including Ave Maria Press, Baker Publishing Group, Baylor University Press, Cistercian, Hendrickson, Templeton Foundation, and Westminster/John Knox.

For about twenty of Claire's years, until her retirement in 2007, Jane Mulder was assistant treasurer. Like many Eerdmans employees, she had begun as a part-timer and eventually worked her way into a full-time job. "Jane and I had a lot in common and were a very compatible team," says Claire. "We came from very similar backgrounds and shared the same work ethic. Like me, Jane worked in various positions at Eerdmans during her thirty-year career. That broad experience is extremely helpful when you take on a financial role." Among her primary responsibilities were human resources, payroll, royalties, and overseeing the accounts payable function.

"Bill and I work together pretty well," Claire says about his boss. "Even when you don't see eye to eye, Bill respects you for saying what you think. If he's considering a project that may not provide what would ordinarily be considered an adequate financial contribution, I may challenge it or express concern. In such cases, Bill always listens to my viewpoint with respect. That sense of respect is very important. In the end, of course, he makes the final decision, but I believe he expects and deserves my considered judgment."

Karl Eerdmans, Bill and Anita's son, keeps a close eye on cash flow. He has a healthy respect for what comes in and what goes out. One needs, in fact, Karl's approval for expenditures that are in any way out of the ordinary. Fortunately for the company, he continues the circumspection of Hero Bratt and Claire VanderKam, and so he is frequently known to say "No" when sometimes the financial powers-that-be have to stand up and say, "We appreciate what you are trying to do, but not so fast."

The Eerdmans bookstore has a long history, going back to the beginnings of the company; for many years it occupied the ground floor of the Pearl Street headquarters. That store died a natural death, however, and for some years the company sold only wholesale books. Eventually, under the tutelage of Bill's cousin Ben Eerdmans, a new operation was created to sell printing company seconds (books with small flaws) and used books from the editorial wing on Jefferson Avenue. Ben lined a shelf in his office with these leftovers — and then two shelves. Word got out among seminary students, who were always looking for a bargain, and before long a kind of retail space emerged at the northwest corner of the building.

During the 1960s and '70s, Casey Lambregtse turned that space into a sizable retail outlet. Lambregtse was a retired book designer, a loquacious yarnspinner who, in addition to his work for the company, wrote novels in Dutch, the first of which was partly autobiographical and became a Dutch best-seller (see the news item that ran in *Inklings* at the time). He would send camera-ready pages to a publisher on the small island community of Urk, in the Ijsselmeer. With his first two novels, Lambregtse gained something of a reputation among the ultraconservative Calvinists of Urk. However, he decided that his third novel should include some mention of sex, which had been missing in the first two. That third novel was his undoing. No longer lionized, he now became something of a pariah in that community.

Lambregtse also edited a cookbook for the company. At an editorial meeting with the author of the cookbook, Bill introduced Casey as Sauté Lamoreaux, a well-known French chef who had

SUCCESS STORY

Eerdmans Book Designer Cornelius Lambregtse recently published a novel that is fast becoming a best-seller in the Netherlands. Written in Lambregtse's native Dutch, and published by T. Wever of Franeker, the Netherlands, *In Zijn Arm de Lammeren* ("In His Arm, the Lambs") has almost sold out its second hardcover printing after only five months. The novel is Lambregtse's first published book in Dutch, the language for which he has written a learner's manual (*Practical Dutch Grammar*, Eerdmans, 1953) for American students.

The action of the novel takes place in a country village in Holland, where Lambregtse grew up in the 1920's. The main character is Fransje, a little boy who dies of peritonitis before his fifth birthday. "The story is somewhat allegorical," Lambregtse told us, "and it observes the working of the Holy Spirit in the life of a little child." An autobiographical element is also evident, relating to the author's loss of his young son.

The Dutch press has given notice to *In Zijn Arm de Lammeren* with no less than fifteen highly favorable reviews in local and national papers. "Seldom have the soul-stirrings of people who adhere to the old-fashioned, experiential religion been described so incisively and with such clarity," observed *De Merwestreek*, a provincial paper in Holland. Several sources have compared the novel favorably — some praising it even more highly — with the all-time Dutch best-seller, *Bartje*, by Anne de Vries.

Inklings readers conversant with the Dutch language and interested in reading *In Zijn Arm de Lammeren* may order the book directly from Mr. Lambregtse, c/o Eerdmans.

Excerpt from the corporate newsletter "Inklings," 1971

agreed to help with the publication of the book. In the course of the meeting, Bill repeatedly addressed Casey as "Sauté," and, on leaving, the author expressed her delight in having had the knowledgeable assistance of so special a person as Monsieur Lamoreaux. "I miss him," says Bill, "in all his guises."

After Lambregtse's retirement, Allen Sundsmo took over the store, and for many years he was its mainstay, greatly appreciated by local teachers, pastors, and students for his broad expertise in and vast bibliographical knowledge of the books that might be of use to them. He retired at the end of 2009, and at that point Jason Kuiper became the manager.

Eerdmans's new store is significantly bigger than the one on Jefferson Avenue was, though it has about the same amount of shelf

Bookstore interior, 2011

space. But, whereas that earlier store was windowless and cramped, this one is well lighted and attractively laid out. The store carries books from all the major denominational publishers: Westminster/John Knox, Fortress, Abingdon, and Broadman and Holman. It also carries such Catholic publishers as Paulist and Orbis, plus the university presses — Oxford, Cambridge, Yale, Duke, and many others. Then there are the major evangelical publishers, such as Baker, InterVarsity, and Zondervan. And, of course, the store carries every title published by Eerdmans.

The Century Arrives

Memories and Hopes

As the Eerdmans Publishing Company looks to the future, it does so with fond memories and fervent hopes. The company's aspirations, philosophy, and vision have been enunciated by quite a number of people inside and outside the company in the above pages. While those lofty principles are important for institutions — especially publishers — to have, they need to be expressed, embraced, and implemented by humans with their feet on the ground and their heads not too far up into the clouds, and their fingers on the proverbial red pens and computer mice. As Claire VanderKam puts it below, "part of the genius of this company is its unique collection of individuals." A few of the longtime employees — along with some former colleagues — create a verbal collage here.

Allen Myers (Senior Biblical Editor)

I specialize in biblical studies, primarily Old Testament and the Second Temple period (Dead Sea Scrolls, etc.). I acquire, develop, and edit reference works, including commentaries and monographs. I've also done one baseball book on the West Michigan Whitecaps.

My two major accomplishments have been two similarly named reference works: *Eerdmans Bible Dictionary* (Myers, 1987) and *Eerdmans Dictionary of the Bible* (Freedman-Myers-Beck, 2000). I am responsible for the following commentary series: New International Commentary on the Old Testament; Illuminations Commentaries; Two Horizons Old Testament Commentaries; Eerdmans Critical Commentaries; Forms of the Old Testament Literature; Theological Dictionary of the Old Testament; Dead Sea Scrolls and related literature; Dead Sea Scrolls commentaries.

Employees tend to remain at Eerdmans for the long haul, an indication of the collegial atmosphere and a common sense of purpose. I came to Eerdmans in 1975, fresh from a PhD program in biblical and Ancient Near Eastern studies and anthropology at the University of Michigan and having experience as editor of a college newspaper and reporter for daily papers in Lorain and Dayton, Ohio. I was hired for nine months to assist Edgar Smith with the *International Standard Bible Encyclopedia (ISBE),* but somehow have managed to stay on. My marriage to Janice Myers (advertising manager) in 1979 was a marriage made at Eerdmans. It has been a privilege to witness the broadening of Eerdmans's focus and to collaborate with the leading figures in biblical scholarship today.

Anita Eerdmans (Vice President of Marketing and Director of Eerdmans Books for Young Readers)

I started working here in December of 1974 — at age seventeen — hired by my brother, Marlin Van Elderen, who was editor-in-chief at the time. I was the editorial gofer, doing the lowest-level jobs in the department. My first project was checking the massive Kittel index volume, the index to the nine volumes (nearly five thousand pages' worth) of tightly packed reference material — some of it in Greek! — in the *Theological Dictionary of the New Testament.* My task was to

Anita Eerdmans

check every six entries or so, and then at the end of the day to tabulate the percentage of errors I found and report that to my supervisors, who would then determine whether closer checking was warranted. You can't blame me for not wanting closer checking ever to be warranted. It was, without question, the most tedious job of my life.

After Bill and I got married, I took some years off for child rearing, but kept coming back to work, though by then always in the marketing end of things. Among the marketing department efforts I look

"A Mr. Squirrel Nutkin and a Mrs. Tiggywinkle are here to see you."

back on with pride are the launch of our website, www.eerdmans
.com, in 2000 (redesigned and relaunched in 2011) and the launch of
our blog, EerdWord, in 2011, after many years of brainstorming and
planning.

In 2005 the children's imprint was added to my portfolio, and I
find it to be the most creatively challenging and fun part of my job.
And children's book people (publishers, librarians, teachers, and
media people) are some of the best people in the world to work with.

I feel both very blessed and very stressed to be a part of the family in this family-owned business. I am truly proud of the rich history
and of the rich present-day of this company. I am proud to be associated with a company that makes decisions based on content rather
than bottom line. (When people ask, "What's the secret of your com-

pany's longevity?" I sometimes respond, "A great tolerance for not making any money!") But the publishing industry today is going through an existential crisis, and to be a smallish independent company among the conglomerates can sometimes seem very precarious indeed. Having a family business means you never get to stop thinking and worrying about the company; you never get to go home at the end of the day and just forget about it. It sort of sits there at the table with you every night, hovering on the edge of every conversation. Hence the stress!

Claire VanderKam (Vice President and Chief Financial Officer)

Part of the genius of the company is its unique collection of individuals. Their dedication, determination, and longevity make us a stable place; yet through it all there's a sense of fun. It's not particularly driven by a need or determination to make money, but by belief in a project.

The business is both quirky and endearing. We're a leading religious academic publisher, yet we'll do a book on whaling in the Arctic, or one by a pitching coach of the Detroit Tigers, Roger Craig, or on Michigan's Polar Bear Expedition in Russia after World War I, or on the Fokker family of aeronautical fame. In many ways the company is a reflection of Bill's personality and values. He has an antic disposition that sometimes masks a strong sense of identity.

John Walter De Hoog (now Wataru Tenga, Tokyo; Editor at Eerdmans from 1967 to 1978)

I first worked for Eerdmans as an editor during the summers of 1965 and 1966, while I was attending theological school. I became a full-time editor in April 1967, working under Calvin Bulthuis and alongside Marlin Van Elderen. We were joined later by Nola Opperwall and by Jon Pott, who eventually became editor-in-chief. To accom-

Claire VanderKam

modate the growing staff, they carved a small room out of the president's office. Over the years, I was to share that office first with Marlin, then with Jon, and finally with Nola.

William B. Eerdmans Sr. was still alive when I first worked there, but his son had taken over most of the executive functions. Bill Jr.'s secretary and indispensable assistant over the years was Mildred Gritter.

In the summer of 1971, I went to a book fair in Atlanta with then editor-in-chief Calvin Bulthuis. At the airport I overheard his wife reminding him to take his medicine if the pain returned. This was the first I knew of his health problems. We were all soon to find out that he was suffering from pancreatic cancer. He did not last to the end of the year.

Jenny Hoffman (Associate Managing Editor)

I've worked at Eerdmans for twenty-two years, starting here in May 1989, the day after I graduated from Hope College. Before that, I did a summer-long internship here between my junior and senior years at Hope. Mary Hietbrink was my supervisor, and she was a good teacher. She had to be a very patient one as well, since I brought long lists of questions to her frequently.

When I began working here full-time, I started out as a proofreader, eventually doing more and more editing. I now do almost all editing and very little proofreading. I also work with Linda Bieze in managing the editorial department, and I supervise our freelance editors, proofreaders, and indexers. Certain projects stand out in my memory. Of particular interest to me, personally, were *C. S. Lewis: Writer, Dreamer, and Mentor,* by Lionel Adey; *An Expression of Character: The Letters of George MacDonald,* edited by Glenn Edward Sadler; and the recent book *Out of My Bone: The Letters of Joy Davidman.* Eerdmans's connection to George MacDonald, C. S. Lewis, and the Inklings goes back many years, and I enjoyed being a part of those books. I also enjoyed working with Marva Dawn, editing nearly all of the books she wrote for us.

I remember fondly lunches at the Schnitzelbank, whether they were business lunches or department Christmas lunches. The editorial department Christmas parties, nearly always at Jon Pott's home, have been special occasions. When he and Gwen were in their lovely former house, these parties would always involve Ping-Pong, with varying levels of skill but always a lot of laughter.

Klaas Wolterstorff (Production Manager)

I started in 1984, my first day out of college. At Calvin College I was a German major and a Latin minor, plus biology and math. I never had my heart set on a career in publishing.

I don't remember thinking about what I wanted to do after college, but for some reason I was hired as a summer proofreader. They never told me to leave at the end of the summer, so I didn't. It's now been twenty-seven years. I guess I report to Bill, but it's not a formal situation. I don't really have the idea I'm reporting to him. At this company you always feel you have access to the top; it's never a matter of a carefully managed or rigid chain of command, though hierarchical charts may exist somewhere. The company is small enough and congenial enough that essentially every door is open to everyone.

Linda Bieze (Managing Editor)

I began in late July of 2003, so I've been here a bit more than eight years. However, I had an internship here in 1977, just after I graduated from college. That was when I learned how to copyedit a book-length manuscript. Jon took me on as a part-time intern, gave me a manuscript and a copy of the *Chicago Manual of Style,* and set me loose. Periodically he'd sit and talk about the process, but mostly I learned on my own. I didn't get a strong sense of the Eerdmans culture at that time, but I knew that the coffee break (men with beards smoking pipes, just like my professors at Calvin) was an important part of it!

Then I went to grad school, after which I got into educational publishing — editing college textbooks and the like — with companies like Scott, Foresman, D. C. Heath, Houghton Mifflin, and Allyn and Bacon. I started in Chicago; then I went east to Boston. I kept in touch with Jon, who is good at that sort of thing.

Early in the 1990s I was at an MLA conference in Chicago, saw an

Eerdmans booth, and saw their wonderful *Dictionary of the Biblical Tradition in English Literature.* I loved it, talked with Jon for a while, and renewed my sense of what the company stands for. We are not narrowly evangelical, nor exclusively about progressive Protestant issues, but care about concerns of Catholics, Jews, and Muslims as well.

Eerdmans is a company that's not swift to make changes, so I learned pretty rapidly after joining the company not to expect that I could change the way things are done. But I have been able to guide processes, to give them more regularity than they had before. Bill definitely has an instinct for what makes a good book. He also has an instinct for special causes, which sometimes produces books that may not repay their financial investments but that are important contributions to religious scholarship.

It's a big source of pride that the company is loyal to the people who work here. The feeling is mutual, and that's why so many have worked here for so long.

Willem Mineur (Art Director)

Sometime in 1982, when I was a freelance designer/illustrator, I was contracted by Joel Beversluis, Eerdmans's production manager at that time, to put together the layout of the interior of the *Handbook to Christianity in America.* For convenience, I was given a work desk and office space at Eerdmans's premises located on Jefferson Avenue, and I worked closely with the editors assigned to the book. This production took quite a few months to complete, as this was before the computer had started to revolutionize the entire industry.

When I was almost done putting in the final corrections, the art director quit and a position of staff graphic designer was offered to me, which I accepted, and June 6th, 1983, became my official starting day as an Eerdmans employee. Since that time I have been responsible for the design and production of book covers and jackets, magazine ads, promotional materials, and so forth.

Mary Hietbrink (Editor)

This is my thirtieth year at Eerdmans. I came here in a roundabout way. I was at the end of my first year in grad school when Calvin College called me and invited me to teach freshman English. I jumped at the chance; I had always wondered if I would like full-time teaching. I enjoyed that opportunity. But it taught me that writing and language were my first loves, not teaching. Just when I was ready to move on, two editorial positions at Eerdmans opened up, and I was hired. I had no formal training, but I had majored in English at Calvin and at grad school, and had done a lot of editing and proofreading work for professors at Calvin.

On my first day at Eerdmans, I got set up at a desk with a pen, a dictionary, a copy of the *Chicago Manual,* and my first manuscript. There I was — an editor. But could I really do the job? I was terrified and elated at the same time. And my first manuscript was a challenge: a tourist guide to Israel written by Jack Finegan.

Milt Essenburg proofread that book. He came to my office, page proofs in hand, and said, "This is pretty good — but let me show you just a few things." There were quite a few things, actually — but Milt taught me well.

When I came here, we published about fifty books a year; now we publish about three times that many. So we're now a "larger" small publisher. What I appreciate is our continuing commitment to publish good books — and I mean "good" from the argument of the book to its technical correctness to its cover. And what I enjoy most about my job is working with authors at every stage of the process; I've met many wonderful writers over the years. In fact, building relationships with authors and handling their manuscripts with care are two principal ways in which Eerdmans distinguishes itself as a publisher. I think that Eerdmans holds up the banner of quality in an era when too many books are rushed into print quickly and poorly, without much regard for either the author or the text.

It's wonderful to be part of a company that's "old-fashioned" in this way — and one that allows its employees to enjoy creative freedom in their work. That's part of what unites us — that's part of the lifeblood of the company. And that's unusual in today's business environment.

Milt Essenburg (Editor)

I began working as a proofreader in 1965. Cal Bulthuis and I agreed that I would do my work according to an order of priorities. Each week he gave me a list, because most of the time I was backed up with work — sometimes as many as ten books were in my room at a time. We worked projects of all kinds. For twenty-five years I proofread *The Reformed Journal;* I laid it out for ten.

Cal taught me most of the editorial skills I have. He was patient with me, since I was trying to get a new start after teaching. When Cal was dying in December 1971, I went to the hospital to visit him, and he gave me a sort of deathbed talk, in which he imagined a bright future for me here.

One of my long-term projects has been The Pillar New Testament Commentary series. I established the general principles, and Don Carson became the outside general editor. The fourteenth volume went out recently. This kind of series is a mainstay for us.

From when I started in 1965 until 1983, an editor edited the manuscript itself (double-spaced), and the whole thing was then retyped by a typesetter-operator. From there, any changes we made (if they were our fault) were charged to us; they were free if they were the typesetter's fault. I always used both red and blue ink: red marks were their fault; blue marks were ours. I'd add them all up and see how much we had to pay.

Hebrew was set upside down and backwards. You had to learn to proofread it that way. The business was entirely transformed by the coming of computers. There are some glitches, but not nearly as much trouble as in the old days. Since 1984, I've rejoiced that things are a bit easier. I'm always amazed that I can send an electronic file

**Milt Essenburg standing in front of a
few of the books he has edited**

of a 900-page book to both Kenya and Australia, and it arrives at both
places in one shot, and with no postage bill.

Glen Peterson

Cal Bulthuis was the editor-in-chief when I started to work at Eerdmans in 1965. He was a very bright man, very mature, calm, subdued, and often apart from the rest of us, who were still working out
our lingering problems of adolescence. Cal was always the voice of
reason.

I always looked to him as my model. For several years after he
died, even after I had moved to Kalamazoo in 1974, I would go to
the cemetery where he is buried, wade through the snow, and
stand in front of his grave and cry. Sometimes I would cry for a
long time. After many years, I came to understand that my crying
was not only for him, but was also for myself and things that I had
lost.

Tim Straayer (Production Editor)

I did some freelance work for Eerdmans, first writing catalog copy and then editing a couple of books, starting in 1982. I was hired as a full-time general editor on April 3, 1983. At the time, I had the distinction of being the only Eerdmans employee who had actually had any formal training in the editorial arts — a one-semester course in editing and publishing that I took as part of my post-graduate work at the University of Tulsa. I remained a full-time editor through much of the eighties, but my time was increasingly split between editing and production matters.

During my first couple of years with the firm, all our books were being typeset outside the company, at a handful of mostly local firms. The company did have one experienced typesetter on campus, Don Prus. Don had worked at the *Grand Rapids Press* as a typesetter, and he had been involved in the newspaper's transition from the old, hot-metal Linotype machines to new electronic and photocomposition equipment. Our book designer at the time, Joel Beversluis, hired Don to get Eerdmans started on a similar transition. At the outset, Don worked on just a couple big projects, most notably the revision of the four-volume *International Standard Bible Encyclopedia (ISBE)*. He operated a big, dedicated console on which he would retype stacks of edited manuscript, adding typesetting specifications as he went along. The console would output this data as a series of holes punched into ribbons of paper tape. He would send reels of this tape off to a typesetting firm that would use them to output galleys on photographic paper. The galleys would be photocopied and distributed to authors, editors, and proofreaders for correction. Don would get the corrected galleys back, type all the changes on the console, send out new paper tape, and start the process all over again. By the mid-eighties, the typesetting firms were charging a dollar per corrected line of type. As I recall, the fee for the type corrections of the third volume of *ISBE* — not the full typesetting bill, but just the corrections — exceeded $25,000. Fees for typesetting the rest of the company's books were proportionally even higher, because we weren't doing any in-house preparation on any of them. It became increasingly clear that we had to change our production methods to bring down costs.

We made the move to in-house typesetting in stages. In a sense, our authors led the way, since academics — and, for some reason, biblical studies folks in particular — were early adopters of the new technologies. We received our first electronic manuscript in 1984. George Goldberg submitted a bunch of floppy disks along with his manuscript for *Reconsecrating America,* and we decided to see what we could do with them. We found a local typesetting firm, The Composing Room, that professed to be able to recover the text on the disks and make use of it. Since Eerdmans had no equipment that would allow us to edit the electronic files before they went to the typesetter, we still had to edit the text on paper and pay someone else to enter the changes into the electronic files, and that didn't leave us much ahead of the game. To get more control over the process, we brought our first personal computer into the company in 1985, a primitive little device outfitted with an early copy of the WordStar word processing program. The computer was set on a little table in the corner of our main conference room and effectively abandoned there. Prior to that, the only computer on site was a mainframe used exclusively by the accounting folks for billing and inventory control. Since we had no IT department, editorial was left to its own devices, so to speak, to figure out how to use it. I was one of the first to start playing around with it, and that almost immediately got me involved in production issues.

One of the problems in the early days of the personal computer was the lack of common standards. There were lots of startup computer manufacturers and software firms, and each went its own way. There were dozens of incompatible physical devices and operating systems and, by the late eighties, over a hundred word processing programs being marketed. Our authors all seemed to go their own ways in this regard, too, using all manner of exotic equipment and software to prepare their manuscripts. I was tasked with finding ways convert this babel into something that our editors and type vendors could negotiate reliably. It took a long time before competition whittled down the number of players in the market.

In 1986 the company took its first step toward using our PCs to set type in-house. Joel Beversluis and I drove down to Chicago to pick up an exotic new device: a laser printer. It was cutting-edge technology at the time, but for all that it was slow and prone to breakdowns, and the print it produced did not begin to match the quality of professional type. But it had the advantage of being cheap to run, and within a year we were using it to produce type for a significant percentage of the less-complicated titles on each list. And, having gotten our feet wet with the laser printer, we were able to make better choices when it came to purchasing more sophisticated equipment. By the early nineties, we were generating our own professional-quality type for virtually all of our books.

During the latter half of the eighties, I had gradually transitioned from the editorial to the production department, though I'm not sure the change was ever formally recognized. By 1991 the dust stirred up by our development of an in-house typesetting capacity had largely settled, though, so I headed back to editorial. I kept my hand in the production game to the extent that I typeset the books I edited, but I was pretty much a full-time editor again.

Things changed again in 1997, when the size of our lists jumped substantially. We needed more hands to deal with the larger numbers of books we were producing, and it was easier to add additional editors (mostly freelance) than to find a new hire familiar with our typesetting software and practices, so I headed back to production. The last book I edited was Reinder Van Til's *Lost Daughters*. I've been in production ever since.

I don't really have a formal job title, but I remember seeing an industry want ad for the position of production editor many years back, and that's the job description I've been listing on my tax returns for quite a few years now. It may speak more to my past in the company as a person with his feet in two departments, though I find that I still get a few opportunities to exercise my old editorial skills on the production end of things.

I'm married to F. William Voetberg, who was a sales rep and then sales manager for Eerdmans back in the seventies. He left to work for AT&T just a few years before I started here.

Roger Van Harn (Editor)

My wife, Ellie, is related to the Eerdmans family. William B. Eerdmans Sr. was a brother to her grandmother, Mrs. Herman Hamstra. Herman Hamstra was a Dutch immigrant who became the importer of Droste cocoa products and related food specialties to the United States. The family lived in Passaic, New Jersey, with offices in New York City. Ellie and I met at Calvin College, and through her I met "Uncle Bill." When he heard that I was preparing for the seminary, he invited us for a visit. He wanted to talk theology.

He welcomed us with wine, cigarettes, and a cigar — signs of hospitality. In their "sun room," full of living greens, we got to know each other. I learned that Uncle Bill cared deeply about good theology and the church of Jesus Christ. In his publishing vocation he cared about blending scholarship, ecumenism, and evangelism.

In my many visits with him, he expressed an ecumenical vision that went far beyond what the church of his time espoused. He asked diagnostic questions to find out what I believed. He wondered if I had any basis for hoping to see Plato in heaven, or if I believed that Walter Reuther was a servant of God. Uncle Bill Eerdmans could speak candidly without sacrificing friendship.

When I was a seminary student, I preached one Sunday for his church. The text was Jesus' words in John 8:31-32: "If you continue in my word, you are truly my disciples; and you will know the truth, and the truth will make you free." It was a "masterful" sermon by my academic standards. Uncle Bill, however, met me in the church aisle as I left the pulpit. He was gentle when he asked, "How many books have you read on discipleship?" That started a long discussion — but later.

Besides my friendship with the Eerdmans family while we were members of the same congregation, Marlin Van Elderen was a valued friend — and also an elder for many years — when I was the pastor at Grace Christian Reformed Church in the inner city of Grand Rapids. While he was untangling the issues of race and gender in society and the publishing world, he was also shepherding our congregation through days of conflict resolution.

Besides our relationship through family and church, Uncle Bill hired me to sell Eerdmans books during my student days at seminary, 1954-57. All of these relationships, plus my longtime friendship with Bill Eerdmans Jr., led to my working for Eerdmans part-time since my retirement from the ministry in 1998.

Reinder Van Til (Editor)

When I came to work in the Eerdmans Jefferson Avenue offices during the summer of 1974, I had known Marlin Van Elderen since we were in grade school together. He was the smartest person I had ever met; indeed, he was the one who taught me how to edit when we were working together on the Calvin College newspaper, *Chimes*. Before that, back in high school, I had taught him how to play the portable (knee-operated, bellows-driven, suitcase-shaped) organs that we played in tandem at the Sunday afternoon worship services in the Kent County Jail. After completing those liturgical duties, we would smoke Old Gold cigarettes and listen to Ray Charles records up in my bedroom.

I had done some freelance work for Eerdmans (via Marlin) during my postcollege years, but had not yet experienced the Eerdmans "culture." In 1974, when I was trying to finish up a PhD in comparative literature (even though there were no jobs whatsoever for finishing PhDs in literature of any kind), Marlin said that Eerdmans had an opening in its editorial department and could take me on as an editor. Whether that was true — or he was simply offering to help me out during a very bad job market — it was a great opening for me. The atmosphere at the company was welcoming and collegial, and, in addition to Marlin, I knew Jon Pott and John De Hoog from our college years.

I took my first leave of absence from the company (which lasted for eight years) in 1978, and Marlin, Jon, and Chuck Van Hof kept me afloat with editing projects when freelance work became perilously thin. For the past 33 years I have not occupied an office at the company and have worked three-quarters time, full-time, and now half-time. But I have stayed close to the Eerdmans "family," and I have been involved in every aspect of its operation. I have acquired books from well-known and not-so-well-known authors; have written books published by Eerdmans; have copyedited many books, from extremely narrow academic monographs to cookbooks; have helped lay out page design with photos and maps; have written and assembled copy for book covers, catalogs, and ads; have picked up books from the printer and transported them with my bare hands (thus getting to know the shipping room staff); and have sold books to both bookstore buyers and individual professors at conferences where I have displayed Eerdmans books (thus using calculators, credit-card sliders, and the familiar cash box).

In the wearing of many hats, I have come to know what Claire, in his reflection above, calls "a unique collection of individuals" — might I even say, "quirky individuals" — that makes up Eerdmans. I daresay that, in those different guises over these many years, I have met and enjoyed more of the unique "Eerdpersons" than I would have had I been holed up in an editorial office somewhere on the premises.

Of course, setting the tone for all the "quirky individuals" is Bill Eerdmans. His view of publishing as a forum for ideas — sometimes warring ideas and beliefs directed at the same subject — has been articulated in the pages of this book, and that view has fit my temperament perfectly over these thirty-five years and more. Furthermore, I always know that Bill will be open and ready to listen to any project that I may have to propose. In all my remote residences and peripatetic meanderings, Bill has always been the magnet that has kept pulling me back to Eerdmans.

Joel Niewenhuis (Promotions Manager)

Some twenty-odd years ago I was hired to work as the copywriter at the Eerdmans Publishing Company — hard to believe I've been here that long. One thing I soon came to appreciate about Eerdmans was that the company published certain "cause" books because of their intrinsic quality or merit, even though it was pretty clear from the outset that they would never yield a big monetary profit — e.g., the many "social justice" South Africa books published in the 1980s and early 1990s. This corporate propensity for publishing stuff deemed inherently valuable and worthy of being published is variously good or bad, boon or bane, depending on how one looks at it, but it has continued to impress me (mostly favorably).

Over the years I've also come to appreciate the remarkable diversity of the Eerdmans publishing program: its quintessentially eclectic lists, season after season, span a wide religious, theological, ideological spectrum and arguably mirror the peculiar, brilliant, sometimes downright quixotic lot of Eerdpersons who have made up the company during its 100-year history.

Sandy De Groot (Editor)

I have been here for thirty-one years. I started as a production assistant. Because we owned our own printing company, I shuttled back and forth between there and my own office. There were no computers, so that place was a wonderful learning experience about how to produce a book. People who come to work here now have no idea how a book is physically made step by step. That old printing company was like watching an assembly line produce a car. It's wonderful to be in a company long enough to work on the design of the car (or the product — a book in this case).

At first I was a little nervous about our move to this new building. Downtown we had our own self-contained world, with the Schnitz, two blocks of buildings, and so forth. But from the first week I have loved it. The neighborhood is quiet and beautiful, and there are windows everywhere. I love this setting.

Now I'm an acquisitions editor: I develop book projects. Spirituality, peace and justice, and art are the three major areas I work in.

Bill has qualities that have kept this company alive for all these years: he has an artistic, creative mind, with special emphasis on the artistic. As Einstein said, the only really valuable thing is intuition, and Bill has that. He trusts his intuitions and acts on them.

He sees possibilities outside the norm, and that has enabled me to do things I would not have done otherwise. That's leadership of a rare kind. No wonder I love my job. Bill has a clear and very wide sense of the human spirit. He wants to learn from you, not teach you.

David Bratt (Editor)

I have worked at Eerdmans for eleven years now. I arrived here in the summer of 2000, a year after I earned a PhD in American church history. This has proven to be a great place for me to land. It has given me the chance to use and build on what I had learned in graduate school, and it has exposed me to manuscripts that go well beyond history and into fields of ethics, public policy, theology, higher education, and Christian practices. Jon Pott, the editor-in-chief who hired me, was able to see that I could be not just a historian, but a useful editor — and a dilettante.

That Eerdmans would be such a good place to land for a trained historian is a testament to the wide vision of the company. Reinder Van Til started Eerdmans's push into history by pursuing a number of books, including *Ethnic Chicago,* which is still in print today (in its fourth edition). Chuck Van Hof then significantly raised the visibility of Eerdmans among historians with his work on our Library of Religious Biography, which engaged well-known historians to write biographies of leading religious figures that could be used alike in college classrooms and living rooms of armchair historians. Chuck also began our most ambitious history project with our U.S. history textbook, *Unto a Good Land: A History of the American People.* So by the time I arrived, Eerdmans already had plenty of credibility in my first area of training and interest. I have been grateful for the chance to build on that credibility with our history program in the years since Chuck moved on to the University of Notre Dame Press.

Bill Eerdmans has always championed that wider vision of which our history program is a part. While he has said elsewhere that Eerdmans has no real mission statement, he did once give me one that has stayed with me. The Eerdmans list, he told me one day while we were chatting by the photocopier, is "a kind of *samizdat* against the secular culture and the dumbed-down church." The fact that this proved to be a setup for a joke involving elaborate wordplay will surprise no one who knows Bill, but that did not rob the setup of its sincerity. I think that our history program, and that indeed every book I have worked on in my time here, is in one way or another a fulfillment of that vision Bill so pithily described.

Janice Myers (Advertising Manager)

I came to Eerdmans in the summer of 1969, immediately after graduating from Calvin College with an English degree. I was hired by Roger Verhulst and Glen Peterson to be a secretary in the marketing department. My job involved typing correspondence, proofreading promotional materials, finding and pasting up reviews (the smell of rubber cement still brings waves of nostalgia), and being general gofer. I left Eerdmans twice — while my children were young — but I just kept coming back. I returned for the last time in the spring of 1978.

Over the years many of the people I worked with have become my dearest friends. A few moved on, some have retired, some passed away, but several still remain at Eerdmans. Not many companies can celebrate employees' 30th or 40th anniversaries. We've had many such occasions here at Eerdmans, and I think that speaks to the true spirit of this company. I have also had the unique privilege of working with my husband, Allen Myers, who is in the editorial department. We have been able to work and travel together for more than thirty years.

I am still amazed that more than 40 years ago I stumbled into a job and a company that would remain such an integral part of my life for so many years.

Duane Watson (Shipping and Receiving Manager, EDI Specialist)

I wouldn't be here right now if it wasn't for Eerdmans. Bill hired Rich Watson in 1956 (55 years ago) to work in the shipping department. Then Donna Rexford was hired into the mailroom a few months later. Rich and Donna became husband and wife two years after meeting at Eerdmans, and several years later they became my parents. After being married and working for Eerdmans a little over two years more, Donna decided to become a stay-at-home mom and raise us six kids, five of whom have had the privilege to work here at Eerdmans. Rich went on to become the Shipping and Receiving Manager and worked for 42 years, until one unforgettable day in 1998 when he had a major heart attack while on vacation in Florida. I will never forget the kindness of Bill, telling me that I should fly down to be with him and my mother and then offering to pay for it. This is a small part of the kindness that Eerdmans shows to its employees and others. As others have said, there is no closed door here; if you have an idea or an issue to bring up, you are always welcome to talk to him.

After working several years part time any chance that I could, I started at Eerdmans full time in 1989 after graduating from high school. When my father's heart attack prevented him from returning to work, I took over his position as manager of shipping and receiving. One of the many things I love about working here, besides the people, is that you are allowed to grow and learn new areas. I have been able to help implement several new computer systems, some of them good and some that we would rather forget. I started

Eerdmans with transmitting orders and invoices through EDI, even though I still don't think that Bill really understands that orders can be received directly from our customers without anyone actually entering them into the system. I have also been able to grow and direct our ONIX transitions, most recently video-editing an author's interview. As other Eerdfolks say, in a smaller company you sometimes have to put on a different hat every day. That is what makes it fun and interesting working here.

Thanks, Bill, for allowing us to become part of your family.

Michael Thomson (Acquisitions and Development Editor)

I have been working at Eerdmans since 1995. My oldest son was one when I came here, so it has always been easy to remember how long it's been. Sam Eerdmans hired me right out of seminary, where I had also worked as an assistant manager in the bookstore. I learned there that I could work with Sam on putting together reference book sales that the seminary student body would just eat up. Over Chicago deep-dish pizza at an SBL conference, Sam inquired if I would be interested in working at Eerdmans someday. To my huge surprise, shortly after my son turned six months old, he called me and asked me to apply. I worked almost fourteen years in the sales department. Through that time, I moved up and eventually became the sales director. The Eerdmans book list, I learned over the years, is a wonderfully quirky mix of trade and academic titles for readers of all stripes. What other publisher can boast that it has published a book on shipwrecks in the Great Lakes as well as one on the Belhar Confession?

It has been a joy to experience in my career the challenge of sales in a dizzyingly changing marketplace. I have seen the old network of savvy theological book-buyers crumble in the face of large bookstore chains and the tidal wave of online booksellers. Just as I left sales for editorial, the specter of e-books was threatening to further revolutionize the world of publishing. The old familiar and comforting world of the folded, crinkled page gives way to an endless avalanche of downloads and terabytes.

During my time in sales I demonstrated an annoying aptitude for striking up constructive conversations with authors at academic conferences. Eventually, a fairly long list of terrific scholars appeared on our list because I had enough good sense to buy them a drink and ask them to write a book for us. Jon Pott, the editor-in-chief, seemingly abiding by the adage that no good deed ought to go unpunished, took me to lunch and asked me to relinquish my job in sales and to embark on a new adventure. I accepted the offer to become an acquisitions and development editor. The transition from sales to editorial has been somewhat like a reverse metamorphosis, from butterfly to cocoon, as much editorial work is solitary while sales entails lots of contact with other people. However, becoming an editor has allowed me much more time to delve more deeply into the substance of what Eerdmans is all about: furthering curiosity, asking questions, feeding spiritual hunger, and pursuing wisdom in conversation with a wide array of fellow-traveler authors. It is an exciting time in theological publishing! The ecumenical horizon is expanding. There is a profound need to be in serious conversation not only with the Judeo-Christian tradition but also with Islam and the whole pluralistic horizon. I am thrilled to be part of the Eerdmans team as we undertake this journey into the twenty-first century.

Still Working

Bill Eerdmans maintains an antic disposition around the office, a lightheartedness that pervades the entire firm. However, his puckish sense of humor never masks the determination with which he involves himself in every aspect of a very serious enterprise. His personality — both smiling and dedicated — characterizes and energizes his company at every turn, a company that has now been under his guidance for forty-eight years. In the summer of 2011, as the centenary of his company approaches, along with his eighty-eighth birthday, he continues to be involved in a number of projects. In early May, for example, he visited the Abyssinian Baptist Church in Harlem, New York, to spend some time with Rev. Dr. Calvin O. Butts III, pastor of that historic church and president of SUNY College at Westbury. Eerdmans is publishing a history of Abyssinian Baptist, and Bill wishes to maintain ties with the church.

Bill's office is piled high with manuscripts, several of which he's always reading. In May 2011, these ever-changing stacks include an analysis of Clint Eastwood's ethical vision, by Sara Anson Vaux; a new volume in a continuing series of medieval commentaries edited by Philip Krey, the president of Lutheran Theological Seminary in Gettysburg, Pennsylvania; a new commentary on Karl Barth; *A Century of Ecumenism,* edited by John A. Radano; a study of Daniel Ogorodnikov, a Russian religious dissident; and Ryan Noppen's history of the Fokker aviation family, the Dutch manufacturers of the famed combat airplane that played an important role in two world wars.

Bill is also excited about the culmination of a project that has been in the works for sixteen years and has been tremendously expensive to develop: the stunning and comprehensive *Encyclopedia of Early Christian Art and Architecture,* edited by P. Corby Finney, emeritus professor of history at the University of Missouri, St. Louis, which will soon be released.

These manuscripts represent no more than a small slice of the 150 or so titles published each year, but the publisher's involvement is more than symbolic. In his interests and his commitment, Bill exemplifies the company's determination to support worthy projects, no matter how long they may take to mature; and he exemplifies its willingness to take a chance on new ideas — if only to discover where they may lead.

Bill Eerdmans, in a photomosaic made from books he has published

Coda

JON POTT

ditors, especially, are supposed to operate with fine critical de-
tachment, and it is a bit disconcerting to comment on a story so
close to home. Much of it, as I read, clicked nicely into place, if anything at Eerdmans can ever be said to click nicely into place. A good
deal of it I already knew when I picked up the manuscript, and much
else, lost temporarily to memory, came back readily along the way.
Even a number of things I hadn't ever known — the saga of WBE's
disappearing (and reappearing) brother Johannes, for example, or of
Bill's cousin Jaguar Jo — certainly fit the familiar picaresque picture.

One thing that did strike me, however, as someone who has
tended to see the continuities in the company story, is how quickly
and to what degree Bill seems to have changed the direction of the
company when he was handed the reins by his father. The evidence,
as Larry and Reinder note, is impressive from the catalogs of the
time. I guess I knew this but underestimated it and took it for
granted. By the time I came along in the summer of 1968, the new
rambunctiousness was already in full cry, and even what might have
been seen as the more fundamentalist excesses of the past seemed
to have been absorbed more as endearing vestiges, part of the fun of
the place, than as embarrassments to be repudiated.

The rambunctiousness of the company had a lot to do with the
tumultuousness of the times. We were reeling from the assassina-
tions of the sixties (Bobby Kennedy was shot the week before I came

207

onboard); even Grand Rapids had had a race riot (during which Bill Eerdmans had bailed a staff member out of jail for violating the local curfew); and the war in Vietnam had landed right on our desks in the form of protesting letters back home from Marlin Van Elderen, who had been drafted and wound up in Vietnam. His writing skills — not to mention his virtuosic typing speed — may have been what spared him actual combat. Some general saw what Marlin could do for him on paper and quickly decided that this was how an editor could best serve his country's cause. All of this social upheaval, as Larry and Reinder point out, affected the idealistic, radicalized young staff and caught us up in books we meant to rock the establishment boat.

Where my own particular literary interests were concerned, the likes of Olov Hartman, a Swedish pastor whose fine novels we published in translation, and Rudy Wiebe, a Mennonite novelist who became a celebrated Canadian literary figure, were rapidly eclipsing any memories of *The Sugar Creek Gang.* We were also already, thanks in large part to a warm relationship with Clyde Kilby of Wheaton College and with Walter Hooper, a confidant of C. S. Lewis, in the thick of publishing books by and about Lewis, Charles Williams, J. R. R. Tolkien, and others of the so-called "Inklings" in Oxford, along with Dorothy Sayers and George MacDonald. The beauty of publishing these people at that time, before they became much more popular, is that they offered us a great deal more literary firepower than we would otherwise have been able to command. My dominant memory of my first summer with the company is of Owen Barfield's *The Silver Trumpet* and of the Dizzy Gillespie–like contraption of an instrument Glen Peterson came up with for promotional display at the two summer book conventions, the grandiose plan nearly dissolving, as it were, when the instrument was eaten full of holes by the acid used to give it the needed silver plating.

My very first editorial job was to edit a novel by the sprightly Grace Irwin, a Canadian writer of no mean talent, especially in historical fiction. I also got my editorial feet wet that summer and fall with two or three of the little monographs in our series Contemporary Writers in Christian Perspective. These, too, especially in their attentiveness not only to rather settled Christians like Lewis and T. S. Eliot, but also to racier ones like John Updike, were worlds away from what the company had been publishing a mere decade or so earlier. The series was well underway when I joined the program and the story of our nearly bagging Auden to write on Tolkien was already part of the heady company lore.

I was full of beans then, says Bill in this book. A *lot* of us, recently out of school, were full of beans then, literary and otherwise. In our romanticizing eye, we were at *The New Yorker,* or, in the case of Rog Verhulst, at *Newsweek,* where he had been an editorial assistant for a time. He did eventually, after he left Eerdmans, publish a guest editorial with the magazine, of which he was justifiably proud. But if not *Newsweek* or *The New Yorker* on the brain, then certainly New York, where Glen Peterson had briefly driven a cab while searching for his star, and Harold Van't Hof, our slightly older sales and then marketing director, had worked for a major reprint company, giving him a more worldly exposure to book publishing than the rest of us had.

A few years later, perhaps in the late seventies, it was decided that a little more direction for the company might be a good thing and that a small retreat for a few of us might be the way to address this. We should get away a bit, said Bill. What about New York? And, of course, where else but the Algonquin Hotel of *New Yorker* fame, where, as in a Woody Allen film, the likes of Dorothy Parker might materialize out of the past, or, from the present, a John Updike or Norman Mailer? Mailer, as it turned out, did show up to meet someone for a drink, looking smaller and less pugnacious than I had imagined. As to any direction for the company, two days of earnest discussion of a well-crafted agenda (mainly Marlin's) ended with Bill's destabilizing summation, "Yeah, but any day's a good day to publish a good book" — and we were off to Broadway to see Mickey Rooney and Ann Miller in *Sugar Babies.*

The sheer eclecticism of the Eerdmans list makes a book like this a daunting challenge to write. What exactly have been the guiding principles whereby, say, a colorful 1920's account of a Dutch artist's adventure in the Antarctic on a Norwegian whaler might naturally join a weighty three-volume systematic theology in the Eerdmans fleet? Well, it's the Dutch connection, don't you know. We have, after all, also published Dutch theologians such as G. C. Berkouwer and Harry Kuitert, some of it translated, by the way, by Lewis Smedes, who, by the way, had been one of Cal Bulthuis's closest friends! You see how it all hangs together in this place. Actually, the company does have some pretty strong connections in the past to ships and the sea. Most of our religiously interested readers probably don't know that one of our all-time best-selling books, still very much afloat, is *Great Lakes Shipwrecks and Survivals,* bought over several decades by thousands of cottagers gazing out at these massive bodies of water and wondering what may have gone down just beyond the horizon they survey at sunset. This book is one of many published by Eerdmans in a sideline program of regional books that includes a long established textbook history of the state of Michigan and even books about Chicago, not to mention a book about the Detroit Tigers when they won the World Series in '84. Reinder VanTil has had a fair bit to do with this program, most recently with a book on an underrecognized group of Michigan troops — dubbed the Polar Bears — who fought the Bolsheviks in a frozen Russia after World War I.

Larry ten Harmsel and Reinder have done marvelous work in sewing together the myriad pieces of the Eerdmans story into what is recognizably a pattern, but if the reader detects here and there a certain last-minute editorial stitching-in of details along the way — or worse, knows of a detail that should be there but isn't — we beg your understanding. And if it is your own name that goes undeservedly missing, we can only fall back, as Bill suggested, on the time-honored "you know who you are."

The truth is that Eerdmans has been blessed by an extraordinary network of authors and advisors — many of them loyal friends — in its multifarious efforts to serve its constituencies, mainly the church and the academy. It begins at home, as Larry and Reinder nicely show, in the Dutch Reformed ethos and theological culture that spawned the enterprise. Whatever the changes wrought by Bill in the sixties, the likes of Herman Bavinck and Abraham Kuyper are still very much alive on the list, directly in books in print or indirectly through enduring influence. And before them, there is John Calvin himself, with perhaps more attention now to his own antecedents in the Patristics, especially Augustine. After Bavinck and Kuyper, one can trace the pedigree through, for example, G. C. Berkouwer and Hendrikus Berkhof on the Dutch side and William Harry Jellema, Henry Stob, and others on the American. And from there the lines are clear to Nicholas Wolterstorff, Alvin Plantinga, and many others, some of whom formed the brain-trust of *The Reformed Journal* and contributed brilliantly to it as well as to the Eerdmans book program. Alongside of them, of course, has been the theological colossus that was Karl Barth, who was not *Dutch* Reformed but got the other half of the equation imposingly right, and today is probably the subject of more scholarship on the Eerdmans list than anyone else.

An important feature of the Eerdmans story in the past forty years has been its attachment to a cadre of splendid scholars in this broadening Reformed community, including, beyond those already mentioned, George Marsden and Mark Noll, both of whom had stronger ties to American evangelicalism than did their Dutch-Calvinist counterparts. And as some of these high-profile scholars and kindred spirits in other more or less evangelical schools became, over time, a kind of Reformed and evangelical diaspora into the broader academy, Eerdmans became the beneficiary of this larger exposure. Alvin Plantinga went from Calvin to Notre Dame, as did George Marsden, to be succeeded now by Mark Noll. Nick Wolterstorff went from Calvin to Yale; Steve Evans went from Calvin to Baylor; Nathan Hatch graduated from Wheaton and went directly to Notre Dame, where he eventually became its first Protestant provost. He is now the president of Wake Forest. Allen Verhey has gone from Hope College to Duke, joining his friend (and our friend) Stanley Hauerwas, along with others who are our valued friends and supporters. The list goes on. For his part, Rich Mouw, trusted confidant to me and proud caretaker of the Kuyperian tradition, went in the reverse direction, from Calvin College to the more overtly evangelical precincts of Fuller Seminary.

These scholars, in turn, as ten Harmsel and Van Til explain in their account of Eerdmans' broadening ecumenism, found natural allies among an emerging number of mainliners concerned with recovering what they treasured as classic Christianity, which had in their view too often thinned to the vanishing point in their respective traditions in whatever the discipline, from biblical studies to theology. For Eerdmans this perhaps most dramatically meant Lutherans, but this was replicated in other Protestant communions as well — and among Catholics. Eerdmans, given its mainline moorings in the Reformed tradition and also its close ties to American and English evangelical scholarship, was strategically positioned to encourage and benefit from this growing conversation across confessional lines. And certainly much of our company energy has gone into fostering this emergent new middle ground.

The company owes a great debt to all these scholars who have been its strong support. And to pastors and others as well who have enriched the conversation out of their daily lives in the church. We also owe a great debt to the many initiatives that have fed, and institutions that have supported, the Eerdmans program. The Ekklesia and Pro Ecclesia groups come to mind. The Gospel and Our Culture Network and The Missional Church movements. Those associated with our Lutheran Quarterly books and with the Kuyper Center in Princeton. The Center of Theological Inquiry, also in Princeton. The "Pulpit and Pew" project at Duke. The "Practices" and "Vocation" initiatives sponsored by the Louisville Institute. The Interventions and the Radical Traditions groups. The Calvin Institute of Christian Worship at Calvin and the Center for the Study of Law and Religion at Emory. The Religion, Marriage, and Family program. One can't possibly name them all, and I won't even try to name the appropriate people. One noble exception, because he's been such a genially persistent presence in our office over so many years: Don Bruggink, whose RCA Historical Series keeps us in touch with where we came from. "Watering the roots," some of us call this loving attention to our past.

"Watering the roots" — not a bad reason, we'd like to think, for our publishing this book.

Appendix: Employees as of Summer 2011

President and Publisher
Bill Eerdmans

Editorial
Jon Pott
Linda Bieze
David Bratt
Nancy Collins
Sandy De Groot
Milt Essenburg
Mary Hietbrink
Jenny Hoffman
Holly Hoover
Allen Myers
Craig Noll
Tom Raabe
John Simpson
Michael Thomson
Roger Van Harn
Reinder Van Til

Production
Klaas Wolterstorff
Jim Chiampas

Deb Danowski
Willem Mineur
Tim Straayer
Dean Thorrington

Sales & Marketing
Anita Eerdmans
Jerry Arends
Rachel Bomberger
Carol Bridgeman
Tom DeVries
Becki Dubois
Josh Dykstra
Vicky Fanning
Franklin Goldberg
Debbie Head
Molly House Spence
Amy Kent
Jann Myers
Joel Niewenhuis
Charles Puskas
Karen Shippy
Lara Sissell
David Surbaugh

The Eerdvolk

Shipping Room
Duane Watson
Cherletta Baber-Bey
Dustin Rawson
Cindy Shoemaker
Drew Thompson
David Triggs
Tom Waid

Finance/General Office
Claire VanderKam
Kathy Best
Jan Brander
Karl Eerdmans

Michele Reynolds
Angel Solow

Bookstore
Jason Kuiper
Joshua Schmidt

Eerdmans Books for Young Readers
Anita Eerdmans
Gayle Brown
Jeanne Elders DeWaard
Kathleen Merz
Abbie Roberts